AFTER THE CEREMONIES

T0312484

African POETRY BOOK SERIES

Series editor: Kwame Dawes

AFTER THE CEREMONIES

NEW AND SELECTED POEMS

Ama Ata Aidoo

Edited and with a foreword by Helen Yitah

University of Nebraska Press / Lincoln and London

The African Poetry Book Series has been
made possible through the generosity
of philanthropists Laura and Robert F.
X. Sillerman, whose contributions have
facilitated the establishment and operation
of the African Poetry Book Fund.

Library of Congress
Cataloging-in-Publication Data
Names: Aidoo, Ama Ata, 1942–
author. | Yitah, Helen, editor.
Title: After the ceremonies: new and
selected poems / Ama Ata Aidoo; edited
and with a foreword by Helen Yitah.
Description: Lincoln: University of Nebraska
Press, 2017. | Series: African poetry book
Identifiers: LCCN 2016038735
ISBN 9780803296947 (paperback: alk. paper)
ISBN 9781496201096 (epub)
ISBN 9781496201102 (mobi)
ISBN 9781496201119 (pdf)
Subjects: LCSH: Women—Poetry. |
Feminism—Poetry. | Ghana—Poetry.
| BISAC: POETRY / African.
Classification: LCC PR9379.9.A35 A6
2016 | DDC 821—dc23 LC record available
at https://lccn.loc.gov/2016038735

Set in Garamond Premier by Rachel Gould.

CONTENTS

Helen Yitah

This gathering of poems by Ama Ata Aidoo is an act of recovery (of many poems that were thought lost) as well as a reaffirmation of the scope, diversity, and importance of her poetic oeuvre. The poems were selected to give as wide a representation as possible of her wide-ranging subject matter, her flexibility in style, and the complexity of her thematic and formal concerns. *After the Ceremonies* brings together many new and collected poems written over the course of three decades. The new poems comprise her most recent as well as others that she refers to as previously "misplaced or downright lost poems." The published ones are mainly selections from her two collections, *Someone Talking to Sometime* (Harare: The College Press, 1985) and *An Angry Letter in January* (Coventry, Sidney, Aarhus: Dangaroo Press, 1992), as well as others that appeared in anthologies, journals and magazines.

The poems in this collection are arranged in a way that foregrounds historicity and chronology. Part 1 comprises mainly new poems, together with a few previously uncollected ones, all arranged in a prelude and four other sections. The other sections in part 1 are "Fires and Ashes," "Grieving for the Living," "The National Corruption Index and Other Poems," and "Ghana: Where the Bead Speaks." Parts 2 and 3 consist of selections from Aidoo's two collections, *An Angry Letter in January* and *Someone Talking to Sometime*, respectively. In these two parts, the original arrangement of poems has been maintained.

Aidoo's poetry occupies an important space in her oeuvre, because even though most of her poems were published after she had established herself as a writer through her plays—*The Dilemma of a Ghost* and *Anowa*—her book of short stories—*No Sweetness Here*—and her first novel—*Our Sister Killjoy*—writing poetry was her childhood dream, and she wrote poems and won prizes for them before she began writing in the other genres. In addition, unlike her other works, which portray fictional worlds, Aidoo's poetry is "real" (with all the illusory dimensions of that concept); personal (in the sense of her being willing to unabashedly treat her biography as source material for the themes and ideas explored in the work); and of "this nightmare world" where the persona is,

> just learning to cope
> in places where
> I cannot take anything at all for granted,
> ("An Insider's View")

Not surprisingly, it is in Aidoo's poetry that we see most of her creative and emotional energies. Here, for example, is how she depicts a moment of bewilderment in "Homesickness" when "my memory had slipped away" at a fish market in a foreign land, where she cannot remember the *Fantse* names of fishes that she has known from her childhood. She is forced to confront a "terrifying truth":

> the names and tastes of fish are also
> simple keys to unlock
> secret sacred doors.

> And I wail to foreign far away winds:

> Daughter of my Mother and my Father's Orphan,
> what is to become of me?

> And those like me?

This passage illustrates one of the abiding themes in Aidoo's poetry: exile and the experience of being an immigrant, and the personal, intimate manner in which it is depicted here could only have come from one who has felt it deeply. It demonstrates how her poetry embraces the span of her experience and her cultural reach.

Yet even as her poems plumb her interior life, they also articulate its negotiation with an outside and often complex historical, political, and aesthetic community. This, in part, explains the many and varied sociopolitical subjects that her poetry deals with, ranging from the history of slavery and its role in the fraught relationship between Africa and the Diaspora, to motherhood, love, childhood, friendship, relationships, hope, loss, crime and punishment, politics, family, nationalism, the decolonization process, education, poverty, despair, dreams, happiness, travels, and exile. And these subjects are often treated against the background of shifting personal and communal bearings.

But one thing that has not shifted is Aidoo's radical vein of thought and how it is reflected in her writing. This is why the relevance of Aidoo's poetry should also be seen in the way it positions her to the left of African politics, alongside the anti-imperialists, the nationalists, and the women's activists.

Aidoo started writing her longer works, beginning with *Dilemma of a Ghost* (1961), during the heady days of Ghana's independence, when the nationalist fervor fueled by J. E. Casely Hayford, J. B. Danquah, and Kwame Nkrumah, among others, had been transformed into postindependence euphoria, not only within the country, but also all around Africa and across the Atlantic. As the first nation in Sub-Saharan Africa to win back power from colonial rule, Ghana quickly became a symbol of racial freedom, political and intellectual emancipation, and the unity of black people. This, coupled with Nkrumah's pan-Africanist ideology and agenda, drew many intellectuals to Ghana from within and without the continent. Notable Diasporans who were moved by this spirit to come to Ghana include W. E. B. Du Bois and George Padmore, both of whom lived in Ghana for some time before they died.

Although the independence celebration quickly gave way to

disillusionment and despair as the political leaders betrayed their people's hope for big and beautiful things, this radical vein has remained an integral part of Aidoo's thought-scape. In her prose, drama, poetry, and critical essays, her radical thought and activism are evident in her identification with the ordinary people, as can be seen in her classic collection of short stories, *No Sweetness Here* (1970)—an identification that places her with the left-oriented politicians fighting for equality, emancipation, race consciousness, nationhood, and African cultural integrity. In her poetry, however, it is also seen in the widely recognized icons (mentioned throughout this volume), whom she addresses directly in her poems or to whom she dedicates them. These would include political figures like Kwame Nkrumah, Malcolm X, Sitting Bull, Stokely Carmichael, and Kojo Tsikata and literary figures such as Anna Rutherford, Bessie Head, Flora Nwapa, Chinua Achebe, and Efua Sutherland. These are not just names dropped to impress the reader, but "kindred spirits" whose lives and work connect with Aidoo's at a deeper level. Her poems engage with the full weight of the intellectual significance of these personalities, and this in turn points to the personal, historical, and political import of this book.

As is to be expected, relations across the Atlantic also continue to be a big interest in her work. Thus, Aidoo fractures in her poetry socially censured issues such as slavery and the trans-Atlantic slave trade (which she also invokes in her other works including *The Dilemma of a Ghost* and *Anowa*), together with the complex, timeless questions of inequality regarding race, class, and gender that are implicated in such subjects. This is illustrated in "Speaking of Hurricanes," a poem in which storms hurled "across the Atlantic to / the poor Americas / and the poorer Caribbean" are juxtaposed with the "political and economic tornadoes" in Africa that

blew our hopes
up, down, left, right:
anywhere and everywhere . . . except
forward to fulfillment.

The damage done by Africa's economic and political hurricanes, clinched in the line "blew our hopes," is reinforced by the imagery of uncontrolled and uncontrollable movement. A gender dimension is brought in when Aidoo makes it clear that women suffer the most as a result of the vagaries of these storms, while able-bodied men, who in the days of the slave trade, used to pick cotton on "our conquerors' doorsteps," now sit idle while "African women in various forms of / civilized bondage" are still subjected to "wiping / baby snot and adult shit." In such a world, "Just reckoning the damage is a / whirlwind of sorts."

After the Ceremonies bears testimony to Aidoo's stature, that is, her glaring celebrity as a pioneer writer, and a poet, who has stood out from the crowd of mainly male authors of African origin. As Jane Bryce affirms in the prelude to a recent film in honor of Aidoo, *The Art of Ama Ata Aidoo* (Fadoa Films, 2014), Aidoo "functions as a front-runner, a forerunner, a person who can put on the table a series of issues which contemporary women can deal with, and continue to deal with." Most importantly, as Ngũgĩ wa Thiong'o has declared in a recent personal essay, Aidoo is "a writer of the world in the world" and "a writer for all seasons."

I hope that readers will enjoy *After the Ceremonies* and that this book will generate greater interest in Ama Ata Aidoo's poetry.

AFTER THE CEREMONIES

PART ONE

New and Uncollected Poems

Prelude

For My Mother in Her Mid-90s

Aunt.

Don't ask
me how
I come to address my mother thus.

Long
complex, complicated stories:
heart-warmingly familial and
sadly colonial.

You know how
utterly, wonderfully
insensitive the young can be?

Oh no. We are not here talking adults
who should know better
but never do.

Aunt,
I thank you for
being alive today, alert, crisp.

Since we don't know tomorrow,
see me touching wood,
clutching at timbers, hugging forests:

So I can enter young,
age, infirmities
defied.

Hear my offspring chirping:
"Mummy, touch plastic,
it lasts longer!"

O, she knows her mama well.
The queen of plastics a tropical Bedouin,
she must travel light.

Check out the wood,
feel its weight, its warmth
check out the beauty of its lines, and perfumed shavings.

Back to you, My Dear Mother,
I can hear the hailing chorus
at the drop of your name.
And don't I love to drop it
here, there, and everywhere?
Not missing out by time of day,

not only when some chance provides,
but pulled and dragged into talks
private and public.

Listen to the "is-your-mother-still-alive" greeting,
eyes popping out,
mouth agape and trembling:

That here,
in narrow spaces and
not-much-time,
who was I to live?
Then she who bore me?

Me da ase.
Ye da ase.

I.

Fires and Ashes

Me Pilgrim

for Kinna XII and Esi (Doughan) II

The symbols were there
for all to see
except me:

Security was not in brick and mortar,
but paper.

All kinds:
old dailies,
new journals,
books,

and the endless files and folders.

I girded me with these and maybe
managed to block my view of the world:
its musts and must nots,
its what oughts and ought nots,

the rules,
the expectations,
the censure.

But never mind.

I was not aware of
how others saw me as
I came and went

. . . until now.

You could not afford
to be generous
knowing I would not be around
when you needed me.

You were kind.
So you hugged and kissed me
hello and goodbye
on each appropriate occasion.

For the rest,
you got on with your lives,
the happy details and the grim:

the weddings,
the births,
the funerals.
The latest research concerns,
promotions granted or denied.

And not forgetting
the very serious business of
acquiring creature comforts.
And me myself?

Lacking the solidity of
bricks and mortar,
dependable land,
the glow of gold and
other valuables,

I pack and bind the year's papers,
lock them in one more

tin trunk,
shove it into one more corner
to wait for my next move.

When the neighbors wake up in the morning
I shall be gone . . .

. . . again!

Heathrow Healing

Surely,
between Ghana and Bosnia Herzegovina,
there is some impressive
mileage in letters of the alphabet, and
solid kilometers.

We do not talk of
the ho . . . hum business of language, or
the even more awkward matter of a
so-called rainbow world, and such.

So, Drazen,
where do I place

this caring,
this anxiety that
nothing at all goes wrong,
awry;

that nothing gets lost in translation and transmission;
that nothing ends up

overlooked, misplaced,
lost?

Just when we thought we'd given up on you,
dear "world's busiest airport":

the crowds,
the noise,
the feeling of a general sort that
out here,
one is frankly not much at all,

darling old inefficient Heathrow,
every now, and every then,
you come out with
your magic . . .

. . . and then some.

As the Dust Begins to Settle II
An Afterword, Twenty Years On

For Kojo T

The dust never really settled. It rose higher,
blew farther, and filled
our mouths with
the most awful grit:
clogged up our lungs,
got into our eyes and
blocked our visions.

Until we began to see things
from our masters' viewpoint.
Which meant
in contemporary parlance—that
socialism died

with the crumbled Berlin Wall, and
Glasnost and perestroika
came to occupy areas where
our old ideals had been.

There was a time when
we were absolutely sure
that the right way to be is left!

No more.
Here and now,
it also means
recognizing ourselves as
fast aging, could-have-been revolutionaries,

who look for life's soft cushions
to rest our brittle bones.

So my dear,
where on this earth
would you find sleep
when the cadres
declare of you that
you kept the state intact and
canonized Stability for
just another neo-colonial phase
of our post-colonial era?

. . . and there are fresh twin gods in town, they say, called
Privatization and Divestiture.

So tear-choked babies we now are,
we scream and wail for
our lost innocence
our perished ideals
our knocked-out hopes.

The three-hundred-and-sixty-degree-turn-around
is complete.

. . . and there are fresh twin gods in town, they say, called
Privatization and Divestiture.

Kojo,
we really fell on
very bad times when
those we considered comrades
became
our worst enemies:
jailed, tortured, run of town.
or stayed, but in varying degrees,
got humiliated into submission.

And now,
that unlike those veranda boys and
much-maligned old prison graduates
who came out to
practice what little they knew to preach,
—just poor half-educated patriots really—

we are
sharper,
clearer,

more practical, and
certainly more aware of the demands of changing times . . .

So look at us
freed leftists,
lugging the briefcases of
"Ultra Rightists" and despair.

Ah-h-h
we trail a step behind
archconservatives:
at once fashionably suited, and
ideologically fashionable!

While those of us who chose
exile, forced or self-imposed,
still crawl through the
padded corridors of the West
in search of crumbs and
limp home every now and then
bearing our bundles and burden of
woeful compromises,
to claim privileges
we would rather have died first
—in our other life—
than look at,
much less touch.

And we cringe at the voice of the future
coming down with heavy censure:
". . . and they brought fresh twin gods into town," called
Privatization and Divestiture.

The schools,
low and high,
have collapsed inside and out.

We did not develop our human power
but took energy from its bones, and
made book-learning a
crime for which
to apologize, as
everybody scrambled for
something—anything—to sell, and
none of it "made-in-Here."

Do you remember when
that was our
spoilt-brats' attempt
to poke fun at
our own industrial efforts?

All have been abandoned, sold, and lost.
Only the massive walls of the silos remain.

And those, they say,
now breed
unprogrammed fish,
errant tadpoles, and
baby snakes
who sing a unisoned farewell to
a nation's long-term plans for
food security
the present secured.

My Brother,
if anybody cares,
it certainly is not those
who for their
personal ten percent have killed
rice farming in these parts

so that we would import
rice from all and sundry,

long grain and short, perfumed or not:
such sweet seductive grain . . .

Meanwhile,
quite, quite unbelievably,
the gutters are still open and
ready to swallow—in an instant—
us and or all our children,

forever bubbling with
old and new poisonous filth: a
nauseous testimony to
how sanitary we are
in mind,
in body and our very soul.

Dear Kojo,
yesterday is irretrievable,
tomorrow unknown.

So it seems that these days
we are caught in

a complex confusing current
wondering:

What next?
Which way?
Where?
How? . . .

To a Silk Shirt in the Sun

It was one of those
glazed-over mornings
with a brittle hardness
and killer-sharp edges.

Everything cracked.
Nothing opened.
Not even the wonder of spatial travel
consoled:

assuming
we could have traversed
the rain and the mud,
the "is-there-an-oven-nearby?" sunsheat,

the germs
the bugs
the viruses
the worms

non-performing phones
powerless power
leaky roofs and
sinking floors.

As for our life,
it's turned into a ball of hairy/spiky juju
the sasabonsam that rolled ahead of us,
no matter how fast we ran.

I drowned, or nearly.

Then I saw you, Silk Shirt,
embroidered and elegantly tailored into
a perfect comfy fit,
a reminder of easier places and softer times.

I could not believe such boldness amidst the muck.
Then I saw her, too.

As you ambled from the east and she from the west
toward some definition-defying space,
eyes dancing, lips a-quiver with
joy that dares not name its source,

I breathed and
pinched myself:
happy to be alive
because you are.

After the Ceremonies

For Belle

I

Alors, Ma Petite

The wonder of writing for you is
I could do it in 3 or 4 languages:
smatterings, mind you.

As to the matter on hand,
it's a tale we can tell,

a right rite that was alright
for the bit of paper
signed, sealed, and handed to you
to be used
now,
tomorrow,
always.

Yet,
in all of this and that,
the stone fell when
the matter-of-fact priest
so matter-of-factly
admonished the groom
not to ever dream of mistaking
you for a punching bag.

Honey,
just hearing him speak of such possibilities
sent my poor heart
dropping somewhere
into the bottom of my being.

Given his size and yours,
I could just see me
shuffling and stumbling
in the dark
to some hole or mansion:
—who cares?—Where
he gave you that single blow . . .

To search for, and
scoop up
the you that had been:
mingy bones,
a spoonful of blood,
a sliver of flesh . . .

2

My Child,
if they came for laces and tulle
there were none.

If they came to see
1 Best Man
2 Maids of Honor
4 Bridesmaids
1 Dozen Pages
2 Dozen Flower Girls
they were not there.
No rose petals and powdered sandalwood.
No 6-tired cakes.
No 15 inane speeches.

Watching
your delicate back and close-cropped hair,
I wondered at what point
you foreswore
Madame Pompadour?

Mind you,
that little affair you wore
was glory in simplicity.
Something jade,
something black?

A black wedding dress?

"Hell no!" Not even you and Kinna
can pass that one off,
here!
Though I can hear
incomparable Chanel
creaking in her pewter grave!

3
My Child,
none of all that was
marriage
by most people's reckoning,
says Yours Anarchistically Truly.

Yet
I know that
one Saturday so many moons ago,
you got properly married.

Do you remember the drama?

The drums,
the castanets and all
the songs in polyglot,
the music: ancient and modern,
historical narratives
that spawned good-natured fights,
the jokes,
the laughter,
the drinks,
the food, the food, the food,
                    and

children running in and out
having their whale of time?

Then it was time.

See you and Kwame walking in
in gorgeous
Sahelian unisex cool:
wondrously white, silvery, perfect . . .

That was fun, Ma Belle,
That
Was
Fun.

II.

Grieving for the Living

An Interrogation of an Academic Kind
An Essay

Dear Auntie Efua,

"Auntie" Efua?!
In lieu of
Dramatist Extraordinaire,
Teacher, Enabler, Inspirer,
Impresario Supremo?

So,
how come you could be that addressed
not just by the youth—near and far—
not just by family—close and extended—
but by your peers, too:
academic, intellectual, and sundry other learned ones?

Some industrial,
others mercantile,
but all reverential?

—and not to mention those who politically and otherwise
could, and may have tried, to burn you in a latter day
auto-da-fé.

Now this is a confession of sorts:
some—not all—of us
wondered every now and then
—not loudly or in any unquiet way, mind you,
but perhaps irrelevantly or irreverently—

what in the Creator's name this kind of domestication was all about?
"It's a sign of our respect," we said.

"And?..."
"... and wanting to own up to those
Wondrous nurture-filled Fridays
—mid-morning, late afternoon, details indifferent—
and the sterling honor of such an appellation.

And seeing too that you had
more than earned that right
from mothering a nation across its
right reaches, left banks, northernmost posts and southern shores...
Ow-w-w,
how you had mothered us:
with that [maddening] formidable [self-] assurance,
those humorously luminous and luminously humorous eyes that
sought out
our inner weaknesses
in hopes of setting us straight
not just some day
but right away,

plus that indulgently mocking laughter
so charming and often tinkling with
the sheer wonder at the wonder that you knew
was this earth, us humans, and our lives...

You walked for us too.
And girl, how you walked!

Purposeful steps
down, inside, and along
cold castle and other walls
clutching carefully crafted
weighty-with-wisdom bits of paper
forty hours a day
ten days a week,

to plead and cajole
in the [vain] hope that
someone, but anyone up there—
and they always were up there—
through you
could might would
hear our cries,
feel our pain and
see the neglect of us and
all that held our life's health,
our almost-complete destitution,
and if only for a while,
taste the bitterness of our
despair.

Dear Gold-Nuggets-Giver and Precious Beads Distributor,
Our True Lady Silk of the Slender Arms,

we remember you so sharply
swinging those arms and cutting the breezes with
the grace and the power of a woodland goddess,
striding and gliding
your way to sundry sites of creative construction:
—the classrooms
—the theaters
—the lecture and other halls where meetings were held of great
    national import . . .

All in your effort to build and have "something built."

Me na Oye-Adee-Yie,
you knew us
didn't you?

the incompetence-with-an-attitude,
the envies,
the jealousies,
the boastful lack of confidence,
the glaring ignorance that sought to hide a knowledge of itself,
in negativity, greed, and mindless cruelty?

And not counting out that puzzling viciousness which gloried
only in the ability to deny others any entry through
doors that should have stayed open for
achievements,
or provided exits from
frustrations and
humiliations . . .

But then,
you never gave up on us:
not for a minute.
Knowing as you did
that given half a chance,
we could, and still can, soar
high above our normal human frailties and
make a glowing glittering something of ourselves and our world.

No wonder then that with such knowledge,
you did
Ananse and his daughter
the only way
they should be done today.

Yet you tiptoed through it all
disregarding the no[n]-sense,
forgiving the foolish-ness,

encouraging,
supporting,
affirming.

So what did you think we were going to do without you,
dear Dr. Mrs. Efua Theodora Sutherland?
Not much:
unless you counted our best under the circumstance.

But,
and this is the other confession of sorts,
since we knew
you brooked no spinelessness,
we hope you had some way to know
we called you "Auntie"
only
in lieu of . . .
. . . "Mother," "Teacher," . . .

For Bessie Head

To begin with,
there's a small problem of address:

calling you
by the only name some of us
knew you by,

hailing you by titles
you could not possibly
have cared for,

referring you to
strange and clouded
origins that eat into
our past, our pain
like prize-winning cassava tubers in
abandoned harvest fields . . .

Some of us never ever met you.

And who would believe
that but those who know
the tragedies of our land
where
non-meetings,
visions unopening   and other such
abortions are
every   day   reality?

To continue a
confession of sorts,

"Miss Head" will just not do.
"Bessie" too familiar.
Bessie Head,
your face swims into focus
through soft clouds of
cigarette smoke and from behind the
much harder barriers erected by some
quite unbelievable
twentieth-century philosophy,

saying more of
your strength
than all the tales
would have us think.

For the moment,

we fear and
dare not accept that
given how things
are,

poetry almost becomes
dirges and
not much more.

But
we hold on to knowing
ourselves as daughters of
darklight women
who are so used to Life
—giving it
feeding it—

Death
was always
quite unwelcome:
—taking them by surprise—
an evil peevish brat
to be flattered,
cleaned,
oiled,
pomaded,
overdressed and perfumed . . .

We fear to remember:
fatigued as we are by so much
death and dying and
the need to bury and

to mourn.

Bessie Head:
such a fresh ancestress!

If you chance
on a rainy night
to visit,

if you chance
on a sunny day
to pass by,

look in to see
—how well we do
—how hard we fight
—how loud we scream

against the plots
—to kill our souls our bodies too
—to take our land, and
—feed us shit.

Come
benevolently,
Dear Fresh Spirit,

that rejoining
the Others,
you can tell them
that now more than ever,
do we need
the support
the energy

to create
recreate and
celebrate . . .

nothing more
absolutely
nothing less.

A Taking Care of Our Bourgeois Palates II—

in Memoriam Jean Genoud, Six Years On

Yes, Jean,
it's about you
after the morning's coffee and the ciggi,
face aglow with fresh makeup, and

joie de vivre.

Which notion was clearly invented,
not by the French, but the French Swiss,
to welcome that wild and funny Luden girl,
their bride from across the Channel.

Oui, Jean,
it's about you
with a tipple of whisky-and-water:
milling the garlic and the peppers
to merge with the mustard
all moistened with the oil for
the day's leafy drenching.

Yeah, Jean,
you so seriously labored over
those leaves' décor!
"Quite mad really," I thought then.

So how can I not remember you all my waking hours,
picking as I have to do, the bottled poisons that
I lie to myself are wholesome enough to
dress up some great greens?

No, Jean,
I now know
"am na gud
at tha' kinda thing."

That hit with such a monstrous loss,
I should pull myself together,
dry up my face, and
move on.

Rather, My Dear,
I sit, and keep sat here
among the dying embers and the ashes, and
simply refuse to be comforted.

And not just that.

Forgive me, Jean:

that I also weep enough tears
to dampen down
your newly-acquired wings, and
create a special lake

which threatens to swallow you
all over again,
or at the very least, slow down your progress
as you wade through toward the gates of heaven.

As for those who remind me that
"knowing this particular problem should be half the cure,"

My Dear,
they have not lost you, or anyone
half like you.

Our Very Dear Juliana

Ei Amanfo,
Ampaampa ara de
Juliana de, e . . . e? De den?
Se demara dze aa, na

Ofie gya edum
Nkwansen abo
Edwuma mu asae
Ehum nyinii etu hen.

Please listen, Mrs. Dwemoh,
and listen good:
You were wrong, if you thought
"Your task here on Earth is over," and
"Your work is done," and
all those clever stuff
we *spiel* to console ourselves.

Juliana Esi Boah Bediako Dwemoh
Hen wuraba feefew Julie,
Owo m' de obiara bowu,
Na sesei ara?

Ammpownam Asaase Afi-Yaa,
Ye nyim de owo dze biribiara idzi.
Naaso hen yemu aa, nkye, nam kor yi ara dze,
ebopow, na epuw ama hen:
aa yebohu n' de oye hen Julie nara.

Dehyedehye,
Feefeefe,
Enyigyenyigye:

And mind you, it's not as if
the world is chock-full of
sympathetic hearts,
understanding minds, and
kind and generous souls.

So to lose you, Julie, is to lose one too many.

Obadwenfo, Nyimdzeenyi Juliana,
Owurayer Dwemoh ei
Tsei iyi na tsei n' yee

Se edwen de
W' edwuma aa
Eba asaase yi do de erebeye n'
Aye ewie ntsi na edze n'
Emirkaemiroka
krimkrim
Ohyewdoohyewdo

Resan w'okyir yi aa
Na ono
Boa o!

Where exactly do you think you are going?
Sure, we must also listen to them
who are wiser in these things and in such affairs,
who tell us that we must gracefully let you go.

But gracefully let you, Juliana, go?
How do we do
that?

Akyerekyerefo hon kyerekyerenyi mapa
Se ewia yi,
Schooldan m' aye komm aa
Na yeyim ne siantsir.
Obaatanpa Julie,
Na irigya schoolfo den?

If it is true
there is some remembrance
where you are bound,

then, Fresh Spirit, come comfort your own
bereft bowel-begotten children,
their children, and
and all who held you dear.

Aa, Amanfo,
Hom mbohwe Juliana bi aa
Ose woewu
Ma yereye n'eyi oo!

Juliana (The Translation)

Come near, come round,
My dear sisters
My dear brothers.
Come take a peek, and
Have a glance
Someone is claiming to be dead
And she looks like Juliana!

Here we are, straw on straw,
clutching at each one in the dark,
wondering if it's true, and if it's a fact
which is the ugliest in this news.
If what has been is what now is,
Then darkness is here and may never leave.

The pot is broken for the clan
The house is shaken, its fires long dead.
Hear the screaming tornado,
The boastful roaring hurricane:
at the workplace
in the market,
here by the hearth at home.

Esi Boah Bediako Dwemoh
Our beautiful singular Juliana,
It's true we shall all die one day,
Did you have to leave this soon?

Dear All-consuming Mother Earth,
Voracious, indiscriminate,
Carnivorous cannibal,

We wish this meat you would spit out,
Offer us back our Juliana:
Beautiful
Winsome
Joyous.

Kind and thoughtful Mrs. Dwemoh
Please listen, and listen good:

If you dreamt
You could skip town
Sneak out of our lives
And disappear,
Happy you'd finished
Your allotted tasks,
Then Mighty Mama, think again.
For us your task is not yet done.

Trainer of trainers
The teachers' teacher
We know why
This noon in the tropics
Schoolrooms are silent
The children abandoned.

The wisest counselor
Accomplished crafter
Sower of hope and joy and peace
You cloaked us in love and habiliments.

Good Mother Juliana
Are you sure you want to leave?

Come near, come round,
My dear sisters

My dear brothers.
Come take a peek, and
Have a glance
Someone is claiming to be dead
And she looks like Juliana!

More Bad News

In Memoriam Fred E. K. Gbedemah

... and then this morning
we heard that you too are gone.

Dear hyperactive wanderlust-ing
Gbedemah. In you and Freeman,
we had our campus
David'nJonathan.

So symbiotic you were,
you two,
we had assumed
a familial bond.

So innocent we were.
It sounds like
a dream,
many years on.

Now we know Freeman is the son of
Mfantsefo and
Afro-Caribbean fathers,
his mother, a Princess of Asantse Kokofu:

And really, how far away
can anyone get from Keta and Anloga?
We ask from this teeny bit of earth and sea
they called the Guinea Coast.

Except that
in those truly halcyon days,
we did not care to check on such things.
           You didn't,
                  Freeman didn't,
                         I still don't.

Too bad if others do.

Brother, you are clearly beyond
the confusion, the hurt, and the pain.
And we would rejoice if we could:

Since any way
we play
this game
is a shame,

I'll just do the ostrich shuffle,
refuse to understand or deal.

If others can, fine.

It's their problem.

It was not yours.

It is not mine.

Awoonor? Ebei Oo!!

Amanfo ei,
Hom mbohwe
Kofi Awoonor bi a ose woewu,
ma yereye n'eyi!

Abae, Awoonor,
Na iyi so ee?
Kofi, obi aa ne nua tse ase ma
Onye n' ham, onye n' kon,
Onnkeye de emi aa
Medze ewu, ma merekesie n' o.

Mbaadodowkun Kofi Awoonor
Eben yaw na yekekae ma
mbusu nsu nyinii aa
otse dem abamen hen yi?

Whopei, Nyidevu,
mbofranyinaa-agya Kofi
yegyina kwaa m' ewiaketekete,
ma adzesae edwur hen, na
yereye den ehu hen enyim yie
etu anamon ako fie?

Kofi, se yebisa w' de
Na woara na eroko hen?
Anaa na erekeyeden aa?
Na yeanye wo enndzi ne yei.

Osiande se enntu dem kwanyi aa,
Okyerewfo mapa,
nkye eben okwan na ibotu?

Ebei Kofi, na amandzee aa otse dem yi,
Afetsi reyeden abobo?
Origyina Nkran ha ara aa,
Anaa obotwa m' ako Wheta?

Hen Ewuradze Nyankopon
woara boa hen,
amma yeannkasa entsia wo o,
osiande, yeedzi emia!

Amanfo ei, hom mbohwe
Kofi Awoonor
biaa ose woewu,
ma yereye n'eyi o!

Awoonor, Hmmm ... (The Translation)

Come you My Sister and you My Kinsman
Fetch a chair
Pick up a bench
Here's a sofa
There's a stool.

We need to sit and take a breath
Before we blind our eyes with tears,
Before the dying sun gets lost to us
And the withering day dries in our hands.

My Brother Kofi of the Dancing Eyes:
That mocked in fury and frustration,
In fun with charm and with affection.

We argued
We fought
And disagreed:

Me calmly secure that you were here
In this city or somewhere else
Causing havoc and
Breaking hearts.

I dare not demand of destiny
How we had earned this calamity,
Since one sage or another said
"No one ever was privy to
What passed in the hour of their parting
Between some other one and his Maker.

Nor dare we query where you were going, or
What you would do when you got there.
That would not at all be fair
That would not at all be right.

You were the poet on a mission
To speak your art and
Sing your song.

Poor Afetsi
Dear Afetsi
That your eyes saw what they saw!

Now we fear to ask of you:
Between Nairobi, Accra, Wheta
From where and whose tongue you must borrow
To tell your tale of woe?

Our Mighty God of All Creation
We pray for strength and energy
To hold this cup of misery.

Lest we blaspheme.
Lest we despair.

And you This Earth, Our Dear Mother
From whom we came and shall return,
Help us to sit around to mourn:

This Brother
This teacher
This statesman
This cantor
This poet.

So come you my Sister, and you My Kinsman,
Fetch a chair
Pick up a bench
Here's a sofa
There's a stool.

We need to sit and take a breath.
Before we blind our eyes with tears,
Before the dying sun gets lost to us
And the withering day dries in our hands.

These Days (III)
A Letter to Flora Nwapa

I

Dear Flora,
do you know
just how much
I miss
you
these days?

Which these days,
is constant in hot arguments
in classroom or out,
   with
neophyte
overindulged
much privilege

rather patronizing
sadly silly
misinformed
non-African youths
the world over.

—we shall not mention the "r" word just yet—

who insist to me
—to me o, Flora,—
how Efuru is
"too astute"
"unreal"
"too independent"

"mythical"

not at all like what
they know about . . . us
African women.

My Sister,
it should make you laugh
    or
smile winningly the way
only you knew how
comforting me with: "don't mind them . . .
Ah, Ama, what do they know?"

Ah, Flora, what do they know?

What on earth would anyone know in
these places about
the women
—and men—
you knew so well,
lived, loved, and worked with:
the mothers who bore you,
the age-mates you laughed with,
the sisters you treasured,
those you raised,
the students you taught,
the ones who read you,
whose kids you wrote for,
who wrote for you and whom
you published and for whom
you published?

What on earth does anyone know

—young or old—
who never ever met you and now never will,
(no fat chance) in this hell we call life?

11

And the youths at home?

Sure, they might know what you knew
            but
what use is awareness
imprisoned in chaos and nothingness?

It's the same old different tale:
we've exiled them from our concern,
left them to grow on the world's garbage:
real, surreal, symbolic
global castoffs hastily assembled,
weevily wheat and expired drugs.

My Sister,
Africa's children have been abandoned by us
the so-called living,
the dead,
the indifferent,
the greedy:

who dreaming or awake
don't see, hear, or smell,
don't understand,
don't seem to grasp
    that
power is not
about beating us down and selling our wealth for

kobos only, for pesewas and for cents.
filling our pockets and
the bellies of our kin.

If it comes to that
how many houses can we live in
—even with our relatives—?
How much food can we eat,
how many *grands boubous* can we wear?
Dansiki? Fugu? Busuti? Nkente?
How many young girls can one man have?
How many cars?
How many? . . . How many . . . ? How much? . . .

There you come again, Flora:
"Ama! relax, what else is new?"

What is new, My Dear Sister,
are the wicked advice, deadly methods
to finish off Africa's youth.

The order is in:
starve them out,
educate them less,
house them poorly,
deny them work.

Let them rot.
Let them rot.
Let them rot.
Let them rot where they were born
    or
let them try to run and die.

Oh Flora,
I just wish you were here
to assure me again
that "everything will be okay,
one day, you'll see . . ."

III

Do you know how much I miss you these days,
my friend of skin that came perfectly blended from
a water goddess's cauldron,
lustrous, shimmering, full-bodied? . . .

Did you ever notice your own
arms, hands, and fingers
weaving dainty gestures that gave strength—but barely—
to your low spoken words?

But it was the neck, Flora, it was
that neck
which made strong men weak and frail men brave,
a piece of contradictory African art
long on a short body and
ringed, and ringed,
fantastically ringed.

Then there were all those elegantly impossible feats.
"Only Flora can attempt to scale Heroes Acre
in a tight skirt and high heels"
        —but you did it.

My Sister, out of this imperial language that
we have to deal with, and which
so often fails us when we need to speak of ourselves,
our hearts and other spaces close to us,

someone has plucked
"gracious"
to describe the woman that was you.

How odd to even think of you
only as a being that once was!

Our gracious lady,
Uhamiri's Child,
if it is true
the dead have powers beyond our mortal selves
        then
please, Flora
do not forget
what you untimely left behind:
your belly-begot and
all Africa's children
whose future lies under the boots of those
who have never wished us well.

Flora,
for us now to stop keening is to hope
you will intercede with the
Great Chukwu and Those-That-Went-Before
for that necessary but illusive power
to free ourselves and Those-Who-Come-After-Us.

Please, Flora?!

Ode to Qunu

for Mandela the Methodist

You Nelson
You Christian
You great
You

But wait!
We honor you
not for
the big ideas:

Reconciliation

Forgiveness

Non-Racial ThisnThat

A Rainbow Nation @ Peace with Itself & The World

You know dem big talk?

Do I hear
naughty Evelyn and
the even naughtier Winnie
giggling?

But it's Qunu, Nelson,
it's Qunu.

That yes, beautiful, but
bare, semi-desert, windswept, grassy heath,

a somewhat scrubby *sadie* hillside in the summer,
there
on the eastern side of the Cape of Good Hope.

—Hm!, we knew of the cape, but of whose hopes we always
   wondered—

Where your forebears were exiled
to freeze and dry out,
starved of their hopes their dreams their bodies their . . .
their children and then
just die?

So that those
who deemed themselves
more worthy
of fecund lands would

grab, keep, and till
with your kin's labor to
prosper them, prosper them,
prosper them.

Dear Nelson,
behind the glory and the wonder of your grand exit,
did others see
what some of us saw?

That single giant cactus
that has had a most wondrously relaxed time to grow and thrive?
A brave survivor along with other
dwellers of those hardship kingdoms:

The Kiwano,
Hoodia, Gordinis,

the Tsamma, and the likes of
Witgatbroom?

Ow Nelson,
Onward Christian Xhosa,
Ow Qunu.

The National Corruption Index and Other Poems

The National Corruption Index

I.

REALLY FUNNY NUMBERS

A 21-YEAR-OLD [Editor's emphasis] farmer, Kodjo Nartey, has been sentenced to 12 months imprisonment with hard labor by the Odumase-Krobo Circuit Court for stealing a quantity of smoked fish. *The Mirror*, Accra, Saturday, August 12, 2012.

What's the difference?

My Frien',
the difference
is as plain as the fact that
at 21,
whatever there could have been
of the whole that was his life
was ahead of him, or
should have been.

As
in the future:
later today, and
all tomorrow.

Nothing poetic
here
nothing pedantic
or philosophical.

"And so?"

And so
the state:
though somewhat already
robbed and raped
comatose,

should have
dragged itself up—tottering or reeling—to
give him,
at *21* mind you,
no less than a second chance, and
"Case closed."

Not cruelly and senselessly
slap him with
12 months imprisonment with hard labor
for stealing
150 Ghana cedis, as in
75 American dollars,
smoked
fish?!

Of course, it never was about him.

The difference?

Mon Ami,
the difference here
is as clear as
the fact that
at 61,
much of this other one's life was over,
kaput,
gone into yesterday—

the actively working part of it anyway,
if he ever did one day's honest job for a day's honest pay . . .

So all things considered,
the state
should not have found it possible to
adorn him with
"a one year suspended sentence"

for embezzling in his various capacities, some
75,000,000 American dollars equals those billions of dear poor
    cedis,
from the state already
raped and robbed by him and his kind.
Comatose.

And yes of course, it was always about him.

That, Nyanyo, is the difference.

II.

JUST THIS MORNING

You must not doubt
me or my tale.

Last dawn brought me
my sister's daughter's son.
My *grandson*, as we insist here,
but a *great-grandson*
in places where details matter, and
each human relationship is
clarified like premium ghee,

completely individualized too as a
smooth round pebble in a stream.

He posed his mission
as a great question
needing attention,
some confirmation and
a plain old response:

that
I
assume the glorious task
—the latest, mind you—of
paying tuition for his in-law's son, one of many.

"Why?"

To further affirm, of course,
his position—jobless himself—as
the village
power broker
extraordinaire.

Hail him who would mediator be
'tween me and all,
all who may want to
profit from knowing him
who shares with me
that most sacred of
sacred links:

Blood.

III.

MORE REALLY FUNNY NUMBERS

Having heard others and
checked things out for yourself,
you can now conclude with some authority, that

about corruption,
it's all numbers.
For You that is One,

how many 100s in 40 homes, 3 villages, 4 quarters of 10 towns
    and 4 cities
you think you can "help"?

Equals 3 big questions:
With what?
From where? And
How?!

IV.

ABOUT SINGLE TREES

Dua kor gye ehum aa; obu.
    —an Akan proverb

Dear data of one,
            The wise ones of old cautioned us about
single trees, standing straight, and serious storms.
So, for all the thousands that cry to you,
if *how* points to time,

what means energy, and
from where is about
cash and other solid resources, then
you
can never win.

Full stop.

V.

ALL OF IT

Over there then, 'twas
Charity begins at home.

Over there now, it's
Taking care of numero uno
Primo!

Here, then and now,
no one saw or sees
home as you, or primo anything.
Home is teeming multitudes—
numero mucho plenti-o.

So
you can only
loot the state to take care of your nearest and dearest,
plus all those to whom
you cannot, and should not
ever think of saying no.

And all that
on your way to

looking out endlessly for
the you that is you?

Pity o!

On Reading Jackie Kay

My Very Dear Sister,
too big a shame that
we cannot ingest, as in hog on,
a good poem.

But beginning with you on the Isle of Man,

we should splurge on and slurp up
great rhymes and rhythms,
stuffing our faces with
beautiful sentiments coolly expressed.

We could pig out on those cadences
that break our hearts and gladden them—
succulent odes, romantic lyrics,
sweet and scary kwadwom, spicy oriki:

We will hors d'ourves on haiku,
guzzle on bubbly couplets and quatrains,
gobble up the sonnets, and
their crazy line restrictions.

Yet still and almost sated,
we shall do as the Romans did,

swigswillsip a delicate vintage and
deal with the poetry of praise, of blame, and the fearful *apae*.

Then singing and dancing,
we shall go to town on free verse.
Doing our poetic bacchanalia,
drumming out our verses.

What a global offering?
What a menu?

My Sister,
we would drink and get drunk
with complete abandon
not worrying about

the inches creeping up our hips, or
the sure damage to our livers.

And then, what heaven!

Why on Earth Do I Continue
To Listen to the BBC?!

for Kinna

Between you, Dear Leader V,
power hungry,
old-style Communist *apparachik*,
insufferably arrogant in your certainties,
a latter-day czar without the crown and the jewels,

and you, Steven R,
intemperate and relentless,
old-fashioned Soviet-bashing Cold Warrior,
very arrogant in your certainties,
intemperate in your jealousy:

don't ask me to choose between
the two of you:
I can't, and
I won't!

Mourning Ricci

Amanfo ei
Hom mbohwe Ricci bi a ose woewu,
ma yereye n'eyi!

Mo nua Kwabena,
it was not that you would not
ask me why I would not
talk to you, or that
I refused to sit you down and tell.

After all
you knew, and
I knew:
no apologies,
no forgiveness.

Right?
Right!

So what I regret
is on behalf, not
of me, at all, but ours:
this beleaguered community
and it's young, Ricci.
That there will be
nowhere,

       never now,

       anymore, a

vain, handsome,
asthmatic
Somebody:
pepper-and-salt haired and bearded a

never never old, just aging man,
out of whom
creative ideas streamed
a dozen a day;
whose energies conveyed—among so many others—
Fashion: with a capital *F*.
And not forgetting our
Gem-winning,
hotel-building,
film-making and
general color-charting
Ricci.

Amanfo ei
hom mbohwe Ricci bia a ose woewu,
ma yereye n'eyi

My brother
who loved women.

Did you say
only tall, thin, and
charcoal black? or
medium-heighted and milky white?
short and sepia,
café au lait,
chocolate smooth, or
just clear brown,
the color of
excellent tea, sensitively brewed?

And everyone single one perma-kept, since
no one could ever
find their way back anywhere,
except
back to you.

Armed as they inevitably were
with—or even without—the babies, and
the forever airline ticket!

Amanfo ei
hom mbohwe Ricci bi ose woewu ma
yereye n'eyi o!

Then there was us the sisters:
the bankers,
the lawyers,
the teachers,
the writers,
administrators,
stenographers,

whose talents you called up,

expertise you bought,
wit you loved, and
brains you unapologetically picked, or only
pretended to pick.

Ossei,
you beer-drinking, koobi addict,
irreligious clown of a
bush saint,

where the hell do you think you are going
in such a hurry,
this tropical noon,
leaving so much
chaos, confusion, and naked panic
behind?

Who do you think
will care for your many orphans,
begotten of you
or not?

Who shall pay
your cutters,
your stitchers,
your models,
your typists,
your miners, and
the just-recruited
waiters, cleaners, and cooks?

Amanfo ei
Hom mbohwe Ricci bi a ose woewu,
ma yereye n'eyi!

Listen, Ossei, and listen good:
who told you, that
you can up and leave just-like-that and
not a word to a
woman, man, or child?

"Well,"
we almost said,
"not even you can get away with such disrespect!"

But then
we already know that you have,
Ricci:
Gone beyond our most abject
pleas and exhortations.

Mbaadodowkun Ricci
Eben yaw na ye-kekae ma
mbusu nyinii aa otse dem abamen hen yi?
mbofranyinaa-agya Kwabena
yegyina kwaa m'
ewiaketekete,
ma adzesae edwur hen, na
yereye den ehu hen enyim yie
etu anamon ako fie?

Hen Ewuradze Nyankopon
woara boa hen, amma
yeannkasa anntsia wo o,
osiande, yeedzi emia!

My terrible brother, Ricci,
I had thought that in this city
I could do quite well without you,

but now,
not only am I not at all sure of that,
I know something clear and cruel,
my grief will never have a cure.

Amanfo ei,
hom mbohwe Ricci biaa ose woewu, ma
yereye n'eyi o!

Ghana

Where the Bead Speaks

Ghana
Where the Bead Speaks

My uncle was the prophetic one,
throwing his beads this way and that,
divining, foretelling,
warnings galore, sweet promising.
One eye on the past, four to the future,
half a dozen or more for now.
He was good if the news was good;
for evil news we blamed the beads.

Made from bones
or fashioned glass,
cut out from stones
or beaten brass

It's the many human hours, Sister,
it's the sweat and blood, Brother,
which make the bead a thing apart
from precious diamonds, opals, and gold.

Turn them this way, shake them that way,
see how they shine incandescent,
see how they glow
in a million hues.

Elegant and enchanting bead,
flowered, flawed, folded, or fielded,
you are the true frame of our feasts,
our festivals, fetes, and fiestas.

Give me a bead that's wrapped in joy;
find me a bead to carry my grief.
We sing of beads, and sing with beads;
just see how well they show on us.

Beads are the zeze of our joyous trails,
the ziz of life when all else fails.
Beads are zany, zesty, zingy,
the greatest zaiku, a grief zapper.

Speak to me of beads, Grandma,
speak to me.
Talk to me of beads, Nana,
talk to me.

She brightened up immediately,
she looked at me with a welcome smile.
Grandma pulled up a stool and sat,
she listened well to me and asked:

"You want a tale on beads, do you?
You want a tale or two?
I'll tell a tale or two to you.
But to speak to you of every bead,

in words that sing and dance like them,
you and I shall surely need
more than my life in hours and days,
more than your life in weeks and years.

A million lifetimes is not much
if beads are the theme, the thought, the thing.
We dive for beads, we swim, we float,
we mine for beads, we comb the woods.

Koli beads for the infant
on his wrist and on her waist,
cascades of white beads for the mother,
a very fitting celebrant.

There are beads that are tame
like what welcomed baby here;
there are beads that are wild,
lion's teeth, lightning struck.
And there are beads around my waist,
For only my and my dot-dot's eyes!!

Have you seen my love tonight?
Asked the ardent warrior youth.
Light of step, curved like a bow,
her eyes were wonders to behold.

She was oiled and very clean,
she was powdered like a queen,
she wore a sarong of the purest silk,
her toes were nestled in their thongs.

Have you seen my love tonight?
She who wore gold beads in her hair?
Then the pretty maiden asked,
who has seen my love tonight?

Who has seen my warrior brave?
he had said no more to war,
he had buried his arrowhead.
His girdle was free of blood and sweat.

He was adorned in his very best,
he was oiled like a king,

with beads of silver in his hair.
Who has seen my love tonight?

They welcome us here in the palest white
and bid us farewell in black,
sometimes blue, and brown, and red,
metallic green, or indigo.

There are beads, by far the most,
that are polished, tarred, and feathered.
There are beads, worked over and under,
elegant hued, thin and narrow.

Beads are the zaffered, the zingiest,
the zenith of all great times.

Cool, calm, and forever collected,
clawed, clayed, or colored,
constantly changing, bead
you are the best, you are the greatest.

So don't talk to me of the chevron.
Don't ever talk of it.
Don't break my ears on the chevron.
Don't break my ears!!!

As barter for my life and yours,
no gem on earth could fit the bill.
Not gold, and if not even gold,
then what on earth is chevron?

I dread the chevron.
It was a weapon
of oppression,
and not at all . . . a bead.

Seven whole humans for one bead?
And what kind of trade was that?
A layer each of sand and mud
for the lives of our kinsmen?

So what if it was one and not seven?
One soul for a shiny piece of bead?
This sounds like the greatest greed,
this sounds like utter foolishness!

Don't talk to me of the chevron,
don't even mention it.
Don't break my ears on the chevron,
don't break my ears.

They say that cheap beads prattle,
rattle, and tattle,
but great beads never talk.

Yet if a string of beads is fine,
it sings,
it dances,
it jumps,
and sizzles.

If a string of beads is truly fine,
it can speak in a million tongues.
It will have something for all,
and say the most amazing things.

And every now and every then
every bead laughs out aloud.

There are beads that are smaller
than the hopes of a mean mind.

Though called bodom, as in a dog,
poochy pug, puggy pooch,
bodom beads, they are so big,
they are the elephants of the pack.
They lead the way
and announce the day.

The nature of beads is a mystery,
the how of it, the feel, the glow
of earthly gems: the least and most,
our first and true try to create, to beautify our human selves.

The best of doors to human hearts,
our spirit's window to the world,
beads clothe our woes in vivid color.
Beads like angels plead for us.

Beads can lift the heaviest heart.
And like tea and precious brews,
beads can warm us when we are cold,
and cool us when we are hot.

Blessed are the beads
that bring us peace.
Spare us, O Lord, in this lifetime,
beads of war, chaos, and strife.

No beaded strings of calamities,
earthquakes, floods, and famine.
No veritable tsunamis of woe.
Keep us cool and keep us warm.

For each color in the rainbow,
there is a bead, somewhere on earth:

a million years old, if a day,
or shy in its newness, and done this dawn.

Blue beads, green beads,
yellow beads and grey,
black beads, white beads,
red beads and brown.

You rise from heaps of your own ash
with more of you than ever were.
You, bead, are an awesome one,
you are the phoenix of the years.

Their making uses endless hours,
the how, the when, the what of it.
The wearing is by a billion souls
whichever way, however much, and everywhere . . .

Mined and molten
man-made wonder,
raw organic, or cooked, and dried,
forever treasured, forever prized.

Bettered and bartered,
broken and beaten,
burnt or badgered,
bruised and bloodied

you are the never-left-behind,
oldest, ordered, owned invention.
Pure and precious, polished pearl,
still safe, sacred, scraped, or scratched;

Traded, treated, tough in trouble,
unique, unmatched, unbreakable.

Verdant velvet, virginal as rain,
beads are virile, vestal, vain.

Gilded and golden,
there can be no palanquin.
If you are not sitting with the king,
you are the queen,
the soul, and spirit within.

Beads are deserving,
beads are worthy,
wash me some beads to warm my skin,
a token of love, a gift for my kin.

Hollowed and hallowed,
jingled, jangled, juggled,
you are our life's companion,
the closest friend until the end.

Don't tell me if there were no beads
something else could meet our needs.
Something what? Something where?
Please keep it there, even if it's rare.

PART TWO

Selections from
An Angry Letter In January

As Always, a Painful Declaration of Independence

As Always, a Painful Declaration
of Independence

—For Me

THE PROBLEM
dear friend,
dear comrade,
is not that

I am a woman and
you are a man
—or at least not only that.

Or that
you come from a different quarter of
                    the village
                    the town
                    the district
                    the region
                    the country
                    the continent
                    the earth . . .

The problem was never that
I am black and you are white
—or not only that.

And much as I wish
I had two whole legs
like you, plus a half,

and given my life,
I could even have done
with an extra arm,
a third eye that saw
not just into me but you
and others and things.

I could have loaned you
a little fat too:
to help you through,

those cold mornings at harmattan
and the even colder nights
of your winter.

Friend,
height
was not missed much
except when

I needed to reach the
upper shelves of my existence
from where I would want
—occasionally—
to bring down
my forgotten
hopes,
aspirations,
plans, and projects
to be dusted . . .

When I would wish, fondly,
that I had one such as you
around

with the long arm that
could elegantly reach for
the tree-tops to
pick
the ripest and most
succulent

            successes from the
                skies . . .

Oh My Brother,
the decision to
sever and separate
was not based on the knowledge of me
as a forever dreamer
unable and incapable of handling
the clear world of
take and
take   and
take

while
you could comprehend the
motions of survival and

move with the speed of
a hare in a burning grassland . . .

I am cutting loose, my dear,
for only one reason:

I do not know
where else you go
whom else you meet
           when we part.

I have had to learn that
these other associations
live:
the connections are
             there and tight
the commitments are real
the allegiances binding.
And the reverberations from them
have a way of
coming at me
shaking my foundations
affecting me
negatively.

I have nightmared of
different gatherings
—after we had parted—
where too
you sit at center-stage

where they call up
names to censure
characters to assassinate
plot our on-doings.

And

you do not say anything.

You do not own up to

knowing me well or
our comradeship and
what I thought

was our—mutual—
understanding.

So my dear, my love,
I am gone.
I am through.

I cannot show up for
the meeting tonight or
any other night
anywhere
ever again.

No
My Dear, my friend,

I cannot show up tonight.

I won't be there.

I am gone.

II.

Images of Africa at Century's End

Images of Africa at Century's End

—in memoriam Cheikh Anta Diop, and for John Henrik Clarke,
Ivan van Sertima, Adotey Bing, Aida Brako, Vincent Odamtten,
and by special request, Esi Doughan and Kinna Likimani.

Who was it said
the reason why
you never see
Black Folks properly
e-v-e-r on film or TV
is 'cause White Folks
"find them threatening"?

Whopei! Abae-o-o-o!

We always thought
our beautiful black skin
        was
the Problem.

So
Afia and Ola
Eye-leen, Lola, and Tapu
bleached and blotched
their skins ugly
to please our masters and our masters' servants.

Now
don't come telling me
flat noses,
thick lips, and
small ears

must also disappear
to put the world at ease?

That must explain
why the Princess Nefertiti
and the youthful King Tut
were dragged to
Michael Jackson's beauty doctor
long before
Young Michael was born,

and also why
the Sphinx
who looked like
Great Ancestor King Khafre
is being redone!

We should have known
we were in trouble

the day we heard
a Corsican general traveled to Giza
by way of Paris and a crown
to shoot
the Sphinx's nose off
for not-at-all-looking like
his.

Enfin! Helas!! Mon Dieu!!!

Ebusuafo,
for years
the Sphinx stood
massive eternal

riddled with wisdom and all
very thick-lipped
very flat-nosed.

We never saw him photographed head-on.

But in the year 2020
the New Sphinx will be unveiled
full visage on view
straight nose raised
thin lips tight
and even, maybe, blue-eyed:

a perfect image of the men
who vested so much interest
in his changing face.

You see, *Wekumei*,
when folks figure
you are their slave
your past belongs to them.

And mind you, the Man will try
                    to grab our future too.

Shall we let him?

In Memoriam
The Ghana Drama Studio

> —*For Robert McLaren, who is committed to the struggle and to drama, and Efua T. Sutherland, who birthed.*

When you asked me
whether I felt at home
coming back here,
I first shuddered,

remembering that actually,
the Ghana Drama Studio
was not pulled down.
It was uprooted.

By the time I got there
—just a few days before your question—
they had filled the monstrous hole
the operation left.

The Ancients had said that
home
is where your shrines flourish.
And the Ghana Drama Studio had been
my shrine . . . of sorts.

I couldn't have called it a
white elephant.

It was just an equally rare
white gazelle

which slept under the city nims,
away from the tropical morning glare,
but
poised,
always,
for a cue
to spring into swift precise action.

But the Drama Studio is gone, Robert,
razed to the ground:
to make way for someone's notion of
the kind of theater
I
should
want.

When you asked me
whether I felt at home returning
here,
I wondered how an old campaigner like
you
could have asked the question which
I had learnt—sadly—to expect
from the friendly
        but chatty taxi drivers who
bring me home here in Harare,
        . . . and elsewhere.

And the forever pain around my heart
jumped, roaring for attention.

Because Comrade,
(holy places and their desecrations aside,
and not to mention the sacred duty
to feel at home anywhere in Africa,

and love every little bit of this
battered and bartered continent which
I still, perhaps naively,
call my own)
I had thought folks like you 'n me
had stopped
defining Home
from way way back,
and have
calmly assumed that

"Home"
can also be anyplace anywhere
where someone or other
is not trying to

fry your mind

roast your arse, or

waste you and yours altogether.

Hm???

A Question from the Expatriate Community

*—to Kari Dako, for her good-natured cynicism, and Kinna (IX),
for her edification!*

A propos something or other that
I cannot remember, and
smug in the plans for her own future,

she had asked me
with a frankness born of long friendship
—and short memory, deliberately cultured—

whether
I can see myself
growing old
here?

And I remember you and your clear views on
Ghanaian emigres
the whole world over:

forever
postponing life and living
as we ready ourselves for a beckoning old age
when, as elders of the clan and
our hairs dyed beyond infant black,

we shall sit . . .
after "a little something in the morning,"
"a little something at noon,"
"a little something in the evening,"

. . . admired by siblings and other
ancillary brothers and sisters who
could never have done as well as we
since they stayed at home:

. . . and held with due respect in the caring arms of
their offspring
our grateful nieces and nephews
to whom we dispense
our black-market-supported
favors and wisdoms.

Both—the hard currency and the experience—
acquired from
unspeakable humiliations
in other people's lands.

We shall try then not to remember
the daily insults:
promotions denied,
our children having to move to
harsher climates
in pursuit of education.

Since, as the dependents of foreigners,
—forget how high their grades or
                              how keen their desire—
they simply
cannot get into
the army   or
schools for would-be
doctors
engineers
lawyers.

Our Wife,
the list of exclusions is very long.

But mind you,
all African countries treat
all other Africans
                              from beyond their borders
like shit,
                    or at best, as
flotsam and jetsam.

"My friend,
where were you all this time?
I was asking if you can see yourself growing old here?"

In my mind's eye,
the image of me as
the adored elder of the clan
recedes
            recedes
                        disappears.

I do not tell my friend
what I was thinking.   That
if what I am feeling now is not old age already,
then frankly,
it signifies little
where the real thing finds me.

I shall be beyond caring:

an unprepared
                        un-secured
                                    wanderer . . .

"In any case," I remind her,

"such questions are
 meaningless for those
 who are not at all sure
 they have a choice."

An Angry Letter in January

Dear Bank Manager,

I have received your letter.
Thank you very much:
threats,
intimidations, and all.

So what,
if you won't give me a loan
of two thousand?
Or only conditioned by
special rules
                    and regulations?
Because I am *not*

white
male   *or*
a "commercial farmer"?

(And in relation to the latter,
whose land is this anyway?)

I know that but for what I am not,
you could have signed
                                    away
two solid millions, and
not many questions asked.

Of course I am angry.

Wouldn't you be if you were me?

Reading what you had written
was enough
to spoil for me
all remaining eleven months of the year,
plus a half.

But I won't let it.

I had even thought
of asking God
that the next time around,
He makes me
white, male, and a "commercial" farmer.

But I won't.

Since apart from
the great poverty
                              and
the petty discriminations,

I have been happy
being me:

an African
a woman
and a writer.

Just take your racism
                  your sexism
                              your pragmatism
                                          off me;

overt

covert or
      internalized.

And
damn you!

Speaking of Hurricanes

—for Micere Mugo and all other African exiles

I

My Sister,

Iave you noticed how
around August/September
every year,

Africa
gathers her storms and
hurls them across the Atlantic to
the poor Americas
      and the poorer Caribbean:
Gilbert, Sullivan, Victor, Hugo . . .

blustering, savage, masculine? . . .

Ow,w,w, . . .
the ruination they leave behind!
Leveled homes
torn cables

poisoned water, and
too many lives snuffed out or at best
broken.

Just reckoning the damage is a
whirlwind of sorts.

And we almost thought:
"how clever of Africa!"

Until we looked around us, and
stopped short on our way to jubilation.

11

See!
Africa had always kept
the more interesting of
the commotions for herself.

Years of economic and political tornadoes
                                   on our courtyards
centuries-old gales that
blew our hopes
up, down, left, right:
anywhere and everywhere . . . except
forward to fulfillment.

We know tyrannical and despotic
winds that whisked away some of
our ablest bodies and strongest minds to

our conquerors' doorsteps,

where they

cut cane
pick cotton and
real garbage.

These days, they sit.
African men sit.
Able bodies strong minds and all,
guarding private property or
staring at nothing at all. While

African women in various forms of
civilized bondage are
still and forever wiping
baby snot and adult shit:
bourgeois black or imperial white.

Who cares?!

III

The Slave Trade was only
a chapter, a watershed perhaps, but
really no more than an episode in the hands of
a master tale-performer who knows too well, how
to change the story,
its telling,
its music,
its drums,

to suit his times.

But speaking of very recent events, My Sister,
have you met any of
the "post-colonial" African political refugees

shuffling on the streets of
London
Paris
Washington
Stockholm and
The Hague?

Minds—and bodies—discarded
because they tried
to put themselves to good use?

Please,
don't tell me how lucky they are.

They know. We know.

They are the few who got away

... escaped
the secret governments and
their secret cabinets,
the secret cabinets and
their secret agendas for
the secret meetings out of which come
secret decisions, laws, decrees, orders from
secret army to secret police for
secret arrests
secret torture and
secret death.

IV

Ow My Sister, let me lament
my openly beautiful land and her people

who hide
good things and bad so well,
only decay and shame become
public,
international.

All storms are dangerous.
But I fear most
the ones I can't see
whose shrieking winds are
not heard around the world
                    and
the havoc they wreak
cannot even be discussed.

These Days: I

—for Baaba Roberts

Little Sister,
keep calm,
relax.

Moboso gya. Mammbohwe wo nkwan m'.

It couldn't have been too long
                    ago that
asking
where anyone was
whom we had not seen in years
meant nothing more than

a goodwilled curiosity,
a wanting to know
how the family—close and extended—is,
a way to catch up with The Home News:

—the young women and men
        of the house, which got married
        and to whom;
—who has had children, how many and when;
—which children are in school, in training,
                where and how they do;

—and news of prosperous times,
        promotions
        businesses expanding
        houses getting built
whether they sank the much
                —needed well in
the neighborhood, and
brought light—
—good shining light to
our mother's doorstep?

—and the bad news too
which we don't need but must have . . .

        Oh Dear Little Sister
        things must have changed
        so much so suddenly.

        They must have.
        They must have.
        How they must have!

Or
I should not have read

such panic in your voice,
just by asking
how Big Sister does.

So what, if she is still at home?

When did home stop being the place to be?
When did being at home become
proof of failure?
A life gone wrong?

Should we all fly away?

       Wander?
            Get lost?

Little Sister, your voice
tells me
what I dare not
see
hear
know:

that
these days
home is
what we fear most;
where we think they are,
who can go
nowhere else;

where we get buried while
we wait to die.

Poor us, My Little Sister,
poor us.

Three Poems for Chinua Achebe

1. A MODERN AFRICAN STORY

Yes,
strange as it may sound,
it is true.

I got deported this morning from
my home, my village, my country and the land which
my forefathers and foremothers bled for,
                                        and tilled
from the beginning of time.

My crime?

I look like My Cousin from across the border, and
His President and My Prime Minister
do not see
eye to eye.

Mind you,
My Brother the Professor protests that
theoretically and linguistically,
"it simply doesn't make sense!
No one can ever be deported from
                            their native country."

I was packing as he was talking.
I had no time to stop and tell him to look
around:

in a land where
former freedom fighters

are vagrants, or buy respectability only
by guarding the property for those they mortgaged
their youths to fight against,
the factories and the homes they crawled
at night—in the good old days—to burn . . .

one can be deported from one's birthplace.

And
I
Was.

This morning.

2. QUESTIONS

—for us, "Today's So-Called Leadership"

They say all beings fight to live:

the mole
the lion
the crow.

They say all creatures must fight to be

in the air
on land
in water.

And as for human you and me

we shoot like wild mushrooms
—in the dark—

sneak up like snakes
claw like cats
pounce and trample,

conquer
kill
consume.

Then just go limp: again
like wild mushrooms
—at high noon.

So where do We come in
Who feel bad just to be firm?
damn all else?
do our own nasty thing or two?
And surely,
five hundred years is too long
to take the kicks
without a murmur?

For what
do we still come
with cup in hand,
begging,
pleading, and
endlessly shifting?

Who would have us be human
in a world
of cruel beasts and
even more cruel men?

How dare we trust

when Trust took a vacation
                    —several million years ago—and
never bothered to come back?

Put quite simply,
in whose name do we ever act?

Whose tomorrow do we sell?

3. NEW IN AFRICA: I

Was Pliny serious
when he said:
"out of Africa always comes something new"?

Shamwari, since he couldn't have foreseen,
he couldn't have meant the last 500 years:

when
Time closed in on itself   and
Europe closed in on us,   and
the only new things
we served ourselves   and
our enemies dished to us
were very old potions:

—nearly always violent—and
just warmed over
every one hundred years or so.

As for Africa herself,
conquered
raped
re-conquered
re-raped,

She wriggles still.

So we also struggle on
—clear eyed or blind—
sometimes with song,
often with dance,

and always,
with a prayer on our lips.

Loving the Black Angel

—for Ben Moloise, Alex La Guma and Our Other Fallen Heroes

I always knew
I loved Lucifer.

Don't ask me
why or
how.

Was he not the first rebel?
a champion
who would not
grin grovel scrape creep or
kiss
the original white arse?

Ah, kinsmen and friends,
help me hail my princely fighter
who

betrayed kings and class, and
gleefully smashed a
thousand glittering crowns.

Loving Lucifer should be
easy:
for
his spirit that refuses to get drenched in
stolen milk and
extorted honey . . .

. . . and in any case,
was he not rough, and hairy, and . . .
pitch black?

Is he not
my enemies' enemy
with plenty promis to be my fren'?
An ally come to
toughen my arm as
I seize thunderbolts
from the earth and skies to
smash crush and reduce sweetly smug slave-drivers to
smithereens?

I just love Lucifer
daring doing dancing
through
waterjets
and teargas and
other great open mouths whose
only mission is

forever death.

I certainly should love Lucifer
who refuses to
"take things as they are,"

to whom dissent
with a racist hangman's rope
seems prettier than
touched-pictures of
"the new African bourgeoisie."

"Hold up the photo for better light, my good
neighbor—you know we are already rather dark—
and my dear, as you know, everything in there is
the best that a black man can have
under the circumstances."

They cut you down, Comrade,
and sent your spirit out.
But who says I want another angel
in my already hot heaving heaven?

Don't you see
in teeming celestial camps and
down among the ancestors,
multitudes of relentless impi
forever fighting
as our heroes must?

So
You, La Guma,
You Moloise, and
All You Beautifully Young Deers
whose lives
the real devil daily

snaps:

don't sleep.

As you join the ancestors

don't sleep.

Stay awake.

Keep alert.

For the battle continues.
The struggle clearly continues,
and we must fight:
You below
us above:
until nothing stands
nothing at all stands
that has to fall.

So that
we can rebuild
our lives
our hopes
our cities of gold.

O, I just love you,
Lucifer.

No Grief No Joy

There is
no joy no grief
when
generals lie ill
from
mosquito bites or quake with fear at the prospect of
just
saying "no" to
a guilty thief.

There is no mourning
no grieving when
mild resolves come
dancing in full battle gear.

There is only
confusion and
shame . . .

. . . and fear for what another day might bring.

An Insider's View

—for Kinna VI

Even a self-imposed exile is
another prison.

I opened the gate,
banged it shut, and
threw the key away.
Or just misplaced it.

I thought I could get
that key again and easily
if only I took some time, and
carefully looked.

But in this nightmare world of:

Aliens Compliance Orders
Temporary Work Permits
applications for regular visas
permanent residence requirements
Green Cards,
                    Red Cards and
                                        Blue . . .
. . . Not to mention:

just learning to cope
in places where
I cannot take anything at all for granted,

we know that
other doors out of this prison are open
                                        all the time.
But they only lead to *suminado*:
the backyard
the outhouses
the fields beyond.

So of course

I can run all I want. To
other lands, other exiles.

Going home is another story.

Homesickness

—for Anna Rutherford

I bolted from
the fishmarket:

my eyes smarting with
shame
at how too willingly and sheepishly
my memory had slipped away
after the loss of my taste buds.

—Just like an insecure politician creaming up
                to his boss.

Familiarly in an unfamiliar land,
so strong and so sweetly strong,
the smells of the fish of
my childhood hit hard and soft,
wickedly musky.

All else fall into focus
except the names of the fish

while from distant places in my head

the Atlantic booms and roars or
calmly creeps swishing foam on the hot sand.

But I could not remember their *Fantse* names.

They were labeled clearly enough
                    —in English—
which
tragically
brought no echoes . . .

One terrifying truth
unveiled in one short afternoon:

that
exile brings losses like
forgetting to remember
ordinary things.

Mother,
when next we meet,
I shall first bring you
your truthspeaker's stone:

the names and tastes of fish are also
simple keys to unlock
secret sacred doors.

And I wail to foreign far away winds:

Daughter of my Mother and my Father's Orphan,
what is to become of me?

And those like me?

Two Letters

I. FAMILY

To Baby Ekua Marguerite Prah: III—from Kalamazoo,
Michigan, USA, as I watch a group of our younger relatives
"just talking" on a Saturday afternoon.

My dear Sister,

We have truly
come a long way
to be here.

Trudging the paths of

Bush negroes
House-and-Field Niggers
Wanting-to-pass Octoroons, and

all other colors between
glistening black and
glaring light;

Non-Immigrants
dragged here in chains;
New immigrants
pulled here by
the economics of
the New(est) World Order!

Sister
from this sample crop of our tomorrow:

I see:
one
vulnerable golden nymph,
fighting against engulfing disillusionment
silent, suspicious, watchful;

right by her is she
of the squeaky laughter by the lagoon where
the muddled waters of
old African confidence and
the modern sea of
America's ethnic bewilderments
meet;

facing those two is
she who
along with her generation of
our continent's
multi-origin-ed
multi-loco-ed
children,
struggles grimly but cheerfully,
today as yesterday to
keep her head, and her voice (!) above
so many waters;

finally, look at their *nuabanyin*
an original Atlas
a giant of warm
smooth blackness
laughing outside while
wailing inside against
history's most paradoxical
invisibility.

Oh my dear Sister,

I had no intention when I began this letter,
of depressing you or myself.

So, to be continued.

Yours truly, . . .

2. AFTER AN ARGUMENT

—for Henry Moyama

Dear Henry,

The issue is not that
as friends
you advocate capitalism, and
I trust socialism.

Ndugu,
the tragedy is
that as Africans
we feel compelled to take sides;

that if there is
an exit
from
collective
decay and distress
we have not
found it yet;

that, by the way,
"A Mixed Economy" is
definitely,
decidedly,

not it.

"Every choice bears a price,
  not choosing costs thrice,"
said the Ancients.

Trust them to know!

III.

Women's Conferences
and Other Poems

Just One More Job for Mama

—for Kinna VII

Ajumako ampesi wobo kaw dzi.

The most difficult science on earth is human engineering.
    —F. K. Buah

My Dear Young Woman,

you know how
I have cut and polished
guilt
into a great and luminous
art . . .

on account of
your failings?

your genuine forgetfulnesses?
your pretended lapses of memory and
other faculties?

So, maybe
it was really my fault.

I should
not only have remembered
to let you know
but also
kept reminding
you
over, and over and over again.

That:
—I swear by my wounded knee
Mara mo ndue,—

it's
not only in America
there is no free lunch.

There
isn't
wasn't and
can't be

ANY free lunch
EVEN in Ajumako.

"They told us
our fathers told us
they told us."

For,
even out there
where
the savannah is
still dotted in places with
good timber,
and
on a clear day
the Atlantic melts and shines
teeming with good herrings in August from
bays, coves, capes, and reefs,
where
the poisonous wastes from
our masters' backyards

have not got to them yet(?), and

there are still coconut trees
for which no one really cares
to claim
ownership . . .
. . . yes, even in Ajumako

THERE IS NO FREE LUNCH.

So Child,
if someone,
—my friend or yours—

remembers that
you
exist and
decides on any day for some reason
to
send
you
a book
some b-r-e-a-d
a card to say
hello, or
just plain old-fashioned love,

stop a while
—considering no one owes you
anything at all—and
say a little

"Thank you."

Please?

Please?

PLEASE?

Whom Do We Thank for Women's Conferences?

Here
in this truly
no man's land,

all is fair as understood not in terms of
Penelope's false blondeness but
that which is right and healthy.

Where
we throw
our big
hairy legs and
bottoms that make any Levi's cry for air.

Hairy too are the faces
we acknowledge
—some were born that way—or
as signs of:
the pills we took in,
the wombs we threw out, and
plain

normal
aging.

Yet

ancient graces
walk elegantly tall or
charmingly petite
in celebration pinks and royal indigos . . .
as though the earth itself was
newly found,
the air a discovery.

We were not afraid of ideas.
Not our own.
Not those of others.

Along those corridors and
in those easy days' assemblies,
apologizing for our being was
not on.

We were
Nobody's wives or mistresses.

No one called us
"Mother":
and when some daughters present did,
it was with the clearest mandate that
they picked the fight where we brought it.

We were
only ourselves:
each alone as when we were born, and

shall be, when
we died.

But
living and together,
a true power thing that
searches
researches
solving
resolving...

And as always
sweetly hopeful as
only women can be.

A Young Woman's Voice Doesn't Break. It Gets Firmer.

—for Kinna IV

I remember
you at four
seven or
eleven,

your baby voice:
both real and pretend
telling me
(or rather whining slightly)
how you missed me, and

who had done what to you or said,
while I
had been away . . .

Now
your voice
comes briskly along the wires,
through the air waves and
over the earth

reporting
how alright everything
at home is, and
ordering me to
just relax
and be about the business
I traveled
all the way here for.

And clearly,
if you missed me,
you were not half about to let on.

Young woman,

. . . for I dare not call you "Child" anymore—
may be
when we are into
our normal existences with
their needs and tensions,

I do not notice the
changes that
take place in you.

But when
I am away and
the phones permit,
I do.

The measures of your growth
knock confidently at the
            doors of my perception
announcing themselves in
more than certain terms.

Of course,
we only speak of a data of
one.

But
if yours
is anything to go by,

then surely,
as she grows
from child into woman,

a girl's voice doesn't break:
it gets firmer.

Comparisons II
We Women, Still!

Honestly, Sisters,

there is some elation here
. . . and some bitterness too.

But if you want to find out
how equal
                    even
the more equal ½ of us are,
come see us at any
public library

—after a normal 9–5 working day.

We are there
in our numbers:
multi-racial
multi-national
multi-ethnic.

All middle class of course.

And therefore,
fat.

But since fat is out
                    for the femmes fatales,
the Grease
these days,
is often in the bones,
not on!

—and indulged. Like
favorite house-mice
scurrying through
the catalogs and
chumping up the bookshelves on
what was left

after the feast of the masters:

desperately hopeful too,
that
one day,
overfed on crumbs but
armed with knowledge

we shall be permitted to
catch on:
lost momentum
lost hopes
lost plans
. . . life itself . . .

And our not-so-privileged sisters?

Honey,
they are
still at it: after even a
normal 9–5 working day:

taken up with
what's waiting of the
brutal loads that were
their lives and most painfully
abandoned,

before, long before 9 this morning.

These Days: II

—for Hilary Homans

Last Night
I could not help but recall
how Mother ended
those precious lessons in
personal grooming:

". . . and remember
to keep a cheerful face:
it costs nothing, and
will do you no end of good."

Last night,
staring in the face of
that
special
plague
which
         —the ancients must have foretold—
shall come to
end all human hopes,

You and I
discovered
         —if we hadn't before—

that these days,
a cheerful face is
a hard commodity to come by.

And we moaned about a ruined world
doubly ruined
for our children
by
epidemics of rolling tanks
scuds,
other missile sorties and
the glee of
foolish old men
cheering at skies
exploding into
flowery flames
to
rain
death
       destruction
           despair.

So
it was not easy.
But we tried
    very hard
        to go shopping for
laughter,

as another lightning ripped
through
the darkening air.

A Path in the Sky

I swear
I saw this morning
a path in the sky
where
clouds had parted for an
aeroplane
to pass.

They looked like
they had done what they could:

arranged themselves
in orderly ridges,
like those Amadu used to make for his yams.

No cloud
could really believe it
the first time it occurred.

They too
had thought
they were in
a nicely noisy smoky hot
nightmare . . .

O, those metal monsters
kept coming and going.
Their numbers and frequency
grew rapidly with time.

Until the clouds
too

came to accept that
the world they knew was gone.

So,
now that
such enforced paths are
a permanent feature of the sky

they wonder
how humans who made the
morning fires
        rising
        falling
        retreating,
        advancing
        gliding
        diving
can find it quite possible to

complain
without end about
droughts
        and floods
                and what-else
without end.

The clouds could say it is:

double-think
double-talk
double-everything.

But that too is a human invention!

A Birthday Gift

—*for Mumbi (Mugo)*

Take this gift, My Child,
it is not much.
Just a bowl of petals:

possibly colored,
dried and scented
artificially.

It serves no purpose.

Except to bring
—when the breezes blow where they should,
which is rare these days—

a whiff of
old forest goodness and
modern garden freshness . . . so called.

But enjoy it if you can.

In full knowledge that
it is just the kind of
not-so-useful gift

I would have loved
when I was then as
you are now.

Take this gift,
my child,
it is for you.

A Postcard from My Vacation

—for Micere Mugo (II)

My Sister,

you and I have agreed that
if I had had the money
I should now be
in the Azores.

Or at least, Mauritius.

Soaking in the sun,   and
covering up my arse
with extra melanin, which, thank God,
yours truly does not need.

So I lie here in Njeri's room,

sleeping the fatigue of
years of questionable
upping and downing,
to-ing and fro-ing.

When I wake up, it is
to read what I wish,
not what I must.
Which makes the difference,

and to crunch up
extra calories, which,
more gratitude to God,
yours truly truly does not need.

I suspect that
from the richer and more precise
world of those who know how
to describe us better than we do ourselves,

this is an excellent
Poor African Woman's Holiday.

Thank you for the space,
and so much else.

A Revelation

"Ask whatsoever in my name, and I shall do it."

I saw these words or those amounting to same
in a shop window that promised solace to a
bewildered me and my world.

"What a fantastical promise!" I thought.

So here is to a humbler me who sees:

the point in being God must be the power to
say this, and more, and do.

PART THREE

Selections from *Someone Talking to Sometime*

Of Love and Commitment

Crisis

Counting cowries
clutching crosses:

what faith
only
comes cresting on my tears
amidst
private sorrows and
public despair?

I hug my grief for warmth
a solitary sleeper's pillow.

Yet I could have done with
a bit of yesterday's happiness
marinaded and
matured
to last through a lean
season or two?

But I can
only recall
how
on the brink of fulfillment,
doubt pricked my ears alert
for the sound of tragedy knocking.

Vision bleary with
fear:
speculations fill the hours.

Shall I know
joy,
when it comes again
the next time round?

Of Love and Commitment

—for Omafumi

How did I know?

I knew because all of a sudden, I started doing
things I had never done before,
things I never knew I could do,
things I always knew I should never do.

For instance?

For instance like stopping longer than was necessary
to talk with
his friend after we had said the initial
hellos and how-have-you-beens.

And when
he said:
"This-and-That is at home, and
we just live around the corner,"
changing my mind about the hot comb and the hair grease.

Oh, it says clearly on the bottle:
WATER REPELLENT.

And
What's-His-Name had a little lamb
whose hair was black as pitch.

Of course, it stands to reason that
he should have been larger than
life.
Dido
of the latter days, my Aeneas.

And he
—with his great limbs stretched out
the hair of his beard curled in sleep—
just wondered
if I
could not
go
"natural."

While
I sat and
loved.

He said:
"I have been on this couch, not stepped out
once
since I saw
you last."

I asked,
with concern in my voice:
"Should they postpone the day's committee meeting?
Do not feel guilty, my dear.
You must conserve your energies.

They should be careful and not overstep their bounds.
There is a danger here in the folds of my cloth . . .
Mind you, I am not one for
keeping the people waiting:
but I shall see to it that
we have this one evening to
ourselves."

I went,
knowing
it was
unthinkable that I should go
and he knew it too.

Or why should he have asked later:
"What would you have done if I had attempted to?"

The house was in a quiet neighborhood
with fear or contentment—
I can't say now
whether it was safe or not.

The room was unlived-in,
the guitar—unplayed.

And I
who had
never
been able to look after
myself,
knew
I could
look after
you.

Oh my dear,
how shall I thank you for
fathering
the mother in
me?

We prompted
one another
on the saints and the martyrs,
counting in Nkrumah:

> they say he was a
> Kruman you know.
> What surprises me
> is how they could
> have deceived
> themselves for so long
> trusting a total stranger?

I borrowed his
Malcolm's Autobiography
to read—

Perhaps we mourned
the death of a hope,
perhaps we rejoiced at
the birth of a promise.

Stokely?
Ah yes,
Stokely.

He said to the cop: "I hope you let her in!"
I have wanted to assure him since that

the pig did let me in—who was he not to?

And his 25-year old face shone out with prophetic words.
It still haunts me.

Kwame Ata should not have died.

For where shall I
carry
a double soul
doubly restless,
and an incestuous desire for
my brothers?

The packing took a long time.
Or the talking did.
The night was long and very short.
A new day was being born with the new world
when
we shoved the last item
                    —was it the dead telephone?
                    Or a newly laundered jacket?
                    Perhaps the checkered-gray
                    he wore all summer?

Yes, a new world was being
born with the new day,
when we shoved the last item into the cab.

But the packing took a long time.

Or the talking did.

The night was long and

short.
It was so long,
we wrote
a poem
a short story
three long plays
a novel
finished our formal studies
saw
the kids through school
solved
other personal problems
frustrated
neocolonial scholarship,
and
made
the revolution.

There was not time
enough
to see
what was in one another's eyes.

I hear the thunder
I see the lightning
I hear the thunder
I see the lightning
Is my love's window open?
Is my love's window ajar?
Perhaps the rain gets into his room?

Perhaps the wind blows out his clothes?
Leave the rest of my hair unplaited, sister.
Leave the threads hanging loose.

I must hurry to my love's room.
I must hurry to shut his window.
I must hurry to my true love's room,
before the rain gets in, sister,
before the rain gets in.

Greetings from London

Sissie,

do you remember when
Grandfather severed a leg in
1867
climbing palm trees
so
the machines in
Manchester
would not die for lack of
oil?

That was before
Sitting Bull had to
stand
for the shafts to sink into
Cherokee country.

And now
they say in order that
Mrs. Smith can do the season's
baking,
some arms

should go to
Cape Town after all.

But you and I are too precious to die.

Meanwhile,
I hold a sherry in my hand
eating shit for a shilling
which is not there.

But wake me early, Sissie,
when the drums roll.

And if before then
a splinter from
a shell meant for another
should pierce my head,
gather
up
my brain
for
a Christmas pudding to
Texas.

Three Poems for Atta Britwum

I. GHANA FUNERALS

Surely My Brother,

It must be only
the living

know of
death:
its colors
its smells.

So on whom is
the joke
when
corpses speak of
mourning
widows weeds and
wreaths?

2. NATION BUILDING

It is
the Greatest Goon Show
of-all-time.

When lisping
French of the
Academie and the
English of Her
Majesty.

They try to prove to
those Unreasonable Youths

that it should follow then
if it's
only
the Dead
know of
living.

The national skeletons are
out . . . of
ancient chests and
Nkondo Kese,
exorcised
themselves to

rattle to us from
hollow mouths and
hollower heads, about
Social Justice
Dialogue-ing with Monsters,
The Pill.

Too bad.

Especially as
they were known to be
sages in their
youthful maturity.

"Men with eyes."

"They knew
book!"

We are to blame
we are to blame
we are
                    as usual
                    once again
                    hopelessly
to blame

Since
too soon
babies
babble,

of daddy this
mummy that—
who shall ride
which car to school
smoke trailing out its
arse, its inner
horrors to the wind—

sounds like
a country
we
all
know of!

And our infants
betray a
congenital fascination for
borrowed ideas
unexamined theories,
zealous only of
getting on . . .

Dead,
completely
dead . . .

. . . at fetal stage.

My Brother,
let's just have
—another cup of tea—

And if
this is
the
neocolonial crime
ask for
whose art it was

before the British
stole
                                    it.
Ain't nothing new here yet.

3. A SALUTE TO AFRICAN UNIVERSITIES

Gaudeamus
Igitur:
Thus shall all slaves
be free.

Gaudeamus
Igitur:
Children mature
this
way.

Darling
miniature
nigger—Oxford:

May you survive the years ahead:
prosperous
snobbish
semi-intellectual
semi-everything!

No,
I am not cursing you.

Na merepaa wo
Na maye den?

Besides,
we are all
beginning to learn
the wisdom of those we do
not respect.

For example?

That
you do not
burn
unless you've got a ready-made
edifice
to replace
what you destroy.

Which, of course,
is possible in this
age of

                              prefab
                              papier-mache
                              vinyl
                              homes
in which, the age and the homes by the way,
we are only guests.

Another
symptom of
The Fault.

Yet,
one must confess
some of your offspring
are more than
just
alright
though even
they
are like
baby mutes with
sizzling sounds in their skulls.

Or some, one or two,
are
just
bewildered dreamers
groping
for images to paint
the horrors of their nightmares—

While here and there
a lonely champion-that-would-have-been
foams at the mouth;
trying to
escape
the scene
where
they auction off
the corporate life
only to
the Lowest Bidders.

A sideshow.

The race itself has yet to begin.

But,
the madness of intellect,
was theirs from birth, and
certainly not acquired from you—
who
has yet to mold
one neat figure from clay.

Indeed,
we shall have cause for more
woe
if it is true that those that come after
have got only you and us for a model,
clear
abridged imitation
of someone else's Cancer . . .

And if one is being
unfair,
forgive.

Because it is also true that
Africa,
Earth's Bonded Whore
has so far
bred
your kind and
none other.

But since
honesty hurts
when we let it,

I must confess yet again
that we also possess
just enough guts,
claiming

> knowledge
> intimacy
> kinship

to call
you
alone.

Bitch—

> like your mother.

For Steve Hymer—A Propos 1966

Steve,
when we try
to be fair

> and

objective

> like they

keep
whining at us to be:

such painful
such grudging
admissions
break—

on
who came good-intentioned.

And
we silently cry for
all wonder-face clouded up
by the dust of
bitter history.

As we sit beside
this
latter-day Babylon,
our minds
aching for the respite of
ancient glories gone, and
future miracles unperformed.

Yet
who could have done more with
time flying on complex skates
abreast
fanged doomcasters and

their agents who lick
bloody lips
savoring
               —in advance—the
sweetness of
the fall
for which they had
toiled?

Some brotherhood of man.

While siblings, friends, and
comrades
endlessly fought,
disputed,
bitched
on such
great questions as

where
our well-wishers choose to grow
their
rice.

So that if we still grieve
for you and Roger and
us—the so-called living—
it's only
because
death visits us in more ways
than one,
Stephen.

But enough.

We have been back to the old
campsite.
Not
all the grains scattered
died.

Some have
sprouted too—
fighting their slow way

through sharp thorns
long droughts
brutal fingering and
such
                    and such and
such . . .

Two for Kojo

1. AS THE DUST BEGINS TO
SETTLE—A LONG STORY II

Here-under-the-sun,
where
appearances are the
only things we
dare
count on,

they thought, and
made
me
think
there was
something quite
funny about
some lady, whose
good feeding
oozed through
great open pores
coming to ask for
you.

"As for
Him paa diε . . ."

And they shake their heads
sympathetic.

But I,
refusing to recognize
negative signals,
skipped around
playing girlish
feigning playfulness,
though I smiled and cried inside,
wanting to
tell them
that
from
what

I
knew of
you,
you
couldn't have
meant
any
harm.

No, you couldn't have meant any harm.

Forgetting the legend,
forgiving the scare.

In any case,
they say

no
sugar-loving nigger
can also
ever
be a
Man.

So I
almost laugh
as I stare at this
green
pineapple country, and listen to faint echoes
come to me from you about
sugar and other
immediate sources of
energy.

Okay . . .

That at least should
hold or
freeze the
smile.

Because
I remember too
how
tired
you'd been for a
long time.

But
first, there was
the myth, then
the legend;

now we get
the scare, and have
our doubts.

O My Brother,
as I sit
here in the Prison Officers' Canteen
caught as it is between the four parts of the two sets,
my faith in you
blooms and wilts
wilts and blooms:
as do these
fragile plants and flowers that
some
other
capricious soul had
planted in the
square spaces between concrete slabs to
hang around for the
occasional
drain of
rain.

Meanwhile on the roster for
today,
they say,

out of 2097 persons . . .
                    and the
questions run away from my
mind

Since such a figure
beats my

village
four times or
more.

"My village?"

Perhaps in
places where the
story of the
struggle for
the right to be is the
only
folktale that is
told,
the village is
where
any comrade
stands alive and hot
                    or
lies dead and cold.

121 to work in the fields
14 to appear in court
37 in hospitals
25 await Presidential Pardon
14 condemned to die
1 in the mortuary
In
The
Mortuary!

So
which mother's son
in bondage to the state

Is Doing
What
In
The Mortuary?

Yes
some questions are
too heavy to ask.

So still
wondering
where
you are, I say my brave
farewells to the
genial warders,
who were
still
shaking their heads in
sympathy.

And I
trace my steps
carefully, back to the
comrades
who,

                    between

birthday parties

                  and

wedding receptions, are
busy
so very busy,
debating
the depth of
the clarity of

your
revolutionary commitment.

2. REGRETS

When
the storm was raging and
the rain falling
as though the
earth had
confessed a
thirst to equal her
longing,
she sat
shivering with
more than the
chill of a wet day.

Except that
she had also hoped
he
could see
her from
behind their
stone walls
iron bars and
bayonets;

as she, like
some other lost version of herself
pants in from the river
where she had
tried to wash the
old years away . . .

. . . though hope wastes
like the rag in a
ten-pesewa lamp which
fills a breath with
more soot than light up
even such small spaces
as these.

Who said
silence is golden
could have been right.

If they saw
gold as a
heavy
non-circulating
non-communicating
metal,
dull
in a capitalist banker's vault,
generating
only
strife and misunderstanding,
not permitting
use
touch
love
trust.

And now
she feared
there was only
pain enough to
kill the remnants of a fire that

never smoldered much.

She also tried to sweep away
those unspoken words which
hung—
a dangerous cobweb—
so thick
it could blur
vision and
properly there
to entangle
them
in their separate loneliness of
suspicions.

Desperately
she brought in red earth
to polish the floor;
the better, in good times,
to reflect
such glorious visage
as he carried.

She would always
listen for his footsteps.

And
since dreams can take
time to die,
she prayed
he not only lived,
but even in all that gloom,
he could forgive
himself, and her,

for mistakes made
out of so much desire

to please.

New Orleans

Mid-1970s

... some tropics are cold.

Carolyn

Back in Africa
where peasant farmers
take a holiday of a
Friday
costumed and seated with
drums and
voices a-ready to
receive
relatives from
across the seas
w h o m
they had not seen in
four centuries
        or
three
        or
two
        or . . .

Who cares?

They say
they ask for
your house
        and not
your money.
        And since
a house is no
home without its
hearth and
voices,

it's alright, My Sister,
if to get a
home
we take
four jobs

        or
two

        or
three

           never mind how
many,

        or
sterile.

Though
we fill
those
empty Saturday nights with
the flakes of our youth as
the weeks peel them off,
surely
surely
surely . . .

Yet
dangerous men or no,
the brothers could help
us
set our perspectives
right if
they knew
how.

But our hearts

Bleed, as we think of
How woefully lost
Some of the brothers
Themselves appear to be.

Not their fault either.

It was an
Ill-omened wind that
Blew through
Our town; and
                    we are
still
looking for our
scattered belongings from among
the ruins of the havoc
that it
caused.

But
keep cool, My Sister,
keep cool . . .
—in spite of dangerous men—

A tight body and a
strong mind can
weather
storms,

even though—
sometimes—

our energies seem too
frail

to go
round
all
the relatives who need
must claim
our strength—what there is of it.

With no effort at all,
I think of
you and your sisters
tenderly. And with my
farewells,

I wish
lots of
blessings upon your house
plenty of
laughter within its walls.

For a Zulu in the Bayous

Robert,
now they say
oil is more
precious to us
than
blood.

I believe them.

Since we have acquired

steel heads
iron hearts and
plastic veins.

Yet,
such a spirit as
wills humans to
glorious
softer dreams
sails from
even
the lonely wilderness of
that alien labor camp—

your exile—
and
across the
foggy
murderous
marshes of
this corner of the world
too,
where
our people have
labored
suffered
so long and so
uselessly.

Therefore,
as I return to
Africa,
"Our Black Mother,"

I err
to carry
this bitterness
in my mind
in my soul:

I blame her,
her carelessness,
her generosity
            for
all
our woes,
then and
now.

Not that it helps any.

And though I
refuse
to reason
myself out of
my longings and
loss of
loves that died
before they could be
born,

something tender
brushes me
l i g h t l y
ever so lightly.
And I wonder, if it was
a hand?
a lip?

Mm . . .
It is the memory of
the whole of
you.

Lorisnrudi

My dear,
there are some meetings
must happen
however brief:

inevitable
encounters
born out of
seemingly
senseless
time.

I met you.

And that's
reason enough—

even though
time
has played
her number
on you and
me.

So that
dragging luggage that
refuses to lock
in protest against
your absence,
I stumble
across
forever chilly corridors,
haunted by the
image of speckles of
gray against
a warm rich face—

your hair and
your beard that
I longed to touch
but did not dare.

My Dear,
since
black is truly
beautiful,

and
we
are
black,

beauty
overflows
from you to me
in other forms:

a quiet voice,
a heart

that beats to
fine human things . . .

I?

I wander
along the lines of
unknown
puzzling circles,
touching lives that I
must touch, and
looking for
bushy heads and
hairy faces
with
hints of
gray
that is
set to light
as blackness
lends to
all colors
including
gray—

I shall

              miss you
              miss you
              miss you.

Acknowledgments—with an Apology to Ronald

Therefore,
what
new questions
shall we ask?

Seeing the
answers are
already
so old,
so known?

And they clamor for
attention. Like
ancient
black
women:
used by all
ignored by all,

buried in
unmarked places.

And the fate is
only
a little worse
for whores
than ladies!

decent and respectable
dowried and wedded,

with
children-that-do-well,
the lot.

What does it matter that we
cross
real woods and
wild waters of woe,
jungles of asphalt
other
synthetic kingdoms
factories of death

                    for death
                    to death?

We still come to
villages on
waterfronts, oil-clogged;
banks of rivers that
breed dangerous gifts;
houses of
cardboard and
rejected aluminum sheets
mud.

Jet stalactites hang from
indoor rafters and corn barns,

the passage of normal days.

And
our huts huddle together for
comfort
or
stand alone on

islands formed from the
night's downpour.

We shrivel here
at the edge of the Sahara
with heat, dry dust that buries:

we shrivel there
in the heart of Louisiana
with whimsical winters, wormy and wet.

You can only
go mad,
catch fever,
die.

No one is talking of yesterday yet.

You weep,
angry
you weep
confused

                            that
something of value
should still be here:

kindness and generosity
trying so
very hard to
dance through
needy hands
which were
too soft
to learn the

strict art of
meat-carving.

I
think of a
festive meal with
gratitude.

Not
just for the
grub
which I was too ill to eat,

but for
an invitation from
lonelier wanderers—

a bed to lay a
tired head on;

while from the
big room, your forever—
kitchen,
voices murmur, full with
legends of
islands in the sun
and
tales of other cities.

—The voices murmur on—
deep as the
Africa that is their
fate:

relentless.

III.

Routine Drugs

Routine Drugs I—for Eldred Jones

They had asked me—

a worthy friend and
a loving brother—

to "stop shouldering
the world's troubles,"
—one meaning Africa,
the other women—

                    "learn to
                    laugh and
                    live!"

I grow hot:

thinking that
laughing?

That's easy:
it's all we do instead of
crying.

And since there's
so much to cry about
we laugh and
laugh and
laugh.

                    But
                    living?

You could tell them
that's not easy.

In a real life
in a real world
perhaps.

But here
where
on a bare belly
for less than a cedi,

you gathered
in single pieces and
carried
ten bushels of
solid stones
your four-month-old baby
straddled on
your back,

slipped,
fell
broke your
arm—?

Laughing we do for
fear of
crying.

Living
we don't discuss
here.

Routine Drugs II

I've stayed
through
this night
in dread of
the morning,
the ether,
the table and
the lamps;

when the magician of the
gleaming steel
will dance around
my prostrate form,
watched
you groan the
hours asleep, or
half-asleep.

You reach for
a cool spot to
rest your
throbbing arm, and even more
throbbing
mind:

The swollen breasts that
drip the hammering of
the heart,
your unsuckled infant,
the older kids and
how they would feed
if at all,

while the hand that
fed them
scantily
burns
and rots
for lack of
routine drugs,

and he, the beloved,
the revered,
comes
raging that
you
should have been such a
careless
cow?

As though it was your fault
that . . .

But why go into it?

Gynae One

"Kwaakwaa"
"Yioo yie"
"Kwaakwaa"
"Yioo yie"
"Alatampuwa"
"Yenyim dzi"

Alatampuwa yenyim dzi

Trolley out,
trolley in.
Trolley out,
trolley in.

Getting scraped
lying in
'vestigating only.
Postpartum complications:
tying it up
throwing one out.
Removing it all.

Dying for it
dying with it
dying from it.

Or
just
dying
dying
dying
dying.

Only corner of the
only world
where
water
must surely be
thicker than
blood.

All agony,
no
ecstasy.

For,
he
comes and stands with
a sheepish grin that
tries to
hide the
scowl and
fails.

Often
he doesn't come at all:
"can't be bothered."
Or
he's run to Lagos in
panic and naked dread?

There
she lies,
the lamb.

Rounded limbs:
dimpled cheeks;
dewy lips
parted
in farewell to a
barely
understood
life.

And they said
they didn't know
much about
anything

except
that
there is a God
and

He is a man.

Comparisons—for Rose

You
drop
your weight on a
leg,

with fatigue
with fury.

Searching places for the kids,
queuing for

> sugar, for
> soap, for
> milk.

You
errand on
everyday problems
just like the rest,
nothing big.

I
pilfer glances at you with

envy
reading consoling words on
your lips and
plenty of scolding in
your heart.

I warm at
your concern
to keep my spirits up.
—But
legs are such good things to have.

Kinsman,
I
am the small-time thief
listening along the inner-prison wall.

They say
these early morning shots
only
muffle in the guts of
murderers and such
others as the
powers want
forgotten.

—But
laws do change
in the morning
at noon
in the evening?

Wondering about Him Who Said No
to the Glare of the Open Day

*In memory of my twin brother whom I never knew because he had
been stillborn.*

So if
the mother who bore her
ten
children and lost
five could
declare:
"what can I do? Since
no one
was in at
anyone else's
farewelling to
their God?"

Then how can I dare?

An aging gazelle
slender of shoulders and
eyes
so small
so delicate
you
wonder if
they were molded to
see with
not just stared at.

                                        —To scream.
So who am I to scream?

Yet, I
do rant and rave,
howl at hell and
heaven too,

at how it
was
that
to have two then
you had to labor for four,
and now that you
can have
all of the four,

they
order and
plan
you
for only
one or
none?

It's hard.

My Brother,
since it's
me is doing
the seeing,

I shall tell you of
the glorious things
up here—

of eggs and hammers
snakes
snails
whales and
ants with intestines,
silver chains
the sea.

And cedis that
fly
faster than the
latest dream in
aeronautical concords—

and they disappear
the dreams
disappear like
sparks from
first encounters
in the evening at its
dawn . . .
"Oh let me cry for my end," sang
the shuffling feet at
Noon:
"the starting has been
bad enough."

My Brother,
I shall
dazzle you with
tales
of friendships that last
forever and
divorces whispering in the wind

before
pretty cakes are cut.

We cry for joy.
We cry for pain.

Why not?

Listen, even if there was the most unlikely miracle of
us knowing what we were about some of the time,

they still
marry us in our
shrouds, and
bury us in the fineries of
the wedding day.

And
you shall hear

of schoolchildren
smart
in the morning with
starched uniforms
satchels and
snacks, and
in the evening,
trembling hands
opening freezer doors at
                        the mortuary.
Pepper shoots
do wave their dainty leaves
                        in the wind
on a rainy day, when

fresh graves are
filled with water that we
                    bail out to the

nunc dimittis,
the tomato sandwiched
between broken lives and
the beer.

Brother,
black is the
only color that
glows against itself

So what shall we do if
we let go of
funerals?

I shall
tell you of
real people who sit to
talk or
write
all day about
real people who stand to
dig and
dig and
dig
all day . . .

And there are other
tales of
cold hearts,
envying minds

ugly tongues
and cruel hands . . .

Aching groins.

Aching groins
where they say
lie
all other
million tales
for the telling of
which even
that eternity
shall not give me
time enough.

No,
not time enough.

IV

Reply to Fontamara

Reply to Fontamara I

Take me to a
tropical heaven
where they
dine
in style,
on

iron rods and
recycled
aluminum.

Cocktails of
ashes and
blood:

                             with

broken bottles
the rare tit-bits.

Sure,
it is so
warm and pretty
here:

the shimmering green,
the azure seas, and
golden beaches
that
reflect
the jeweled
toes of

legal thieves and
holy murderers
in
such
ancient golden
gold

purchased
as gold must,
with . . .

Reply to Fontamara II

They know
who suffer snow,
that
in the long summer heat
blood
runs
so easily in the street.

My Brother,
let us sing to
the glories of Fontamara
from here
where
you
and I, and other
poets dwell.

Not
there
where
life must be lived, and
dollars are the dices
that ever roll sixes.

And there are
even now,
great grandfather trees,
those that escaped
the roar of the
chainsaw,
still receiving
nourishment from the
good
old
earth!

But then,
the sun has been up for so long
brother,
we no more
know
the difference between
a mild morning and
a hot noon.
A little cool life could do,
no?
Just
a small cool day?

Now That the Weather Man
Has Gone Crazy . . .

. . . let us take
this bright morning, and
wrap up our dying hopes for
safe-keeping.

What else can we do,

overtaken

     —as we are—

by
winter at the height of an
equatorial noon?

We cannot defend ourselves
against an adversary
we don't know.

And so
we crouch here
in the blazing sun,

shaking with horror at
our teeth—as they
chatter, and
fall, from
frostbite!

Heavy Traffic

Who are they singing of
forever toil and
eternal woe?

It's the
highlife, brother,
come and dance.

Funerals are full of fun.

Death throws the only parties
we enjoy.

When in doubt,
follow me to the
cocoa farm blasted by
last year's drought.
On the way back,
we shall meet and
do good business

                        with

them that
carry
coffins filled with
bangles
bleaching creams

                      and

                      corned beef.

From the Only Speech That Was
Not Delivered at the Rally

Amanfuo,

just look at
us
        and
know
the full extent of
your distress.

Between me
        and
the other candidate,
there's quite a lot to choose from:

an extra inch or so of
bones,
a few pounds' difference—
in weight.

Where one was born is
most important. Especially when
we
tell
you
so.

Do take note

        and

not forget
to give me your vote
along with your
          wife.
I am your tribesman
          and

who else but I,
your own housefly,
can suck your
          sores
to hurt the most?

Education too
must not be missed.

          Or

how could we who have the best
make you and them
who have the least
or none at all
look
small?

For the rest, dear countrymen,
we promise you
no success,
no prosperity.

Man must have something to live for.

We survive on our
failures.

As things
do stand,
I've missed more
chances
       than
I can count,
       or
wish to count.

So
Time gives
me her
"Go-ahead"
to chop you small
before I'm dead.

v.

Legacies

The Visible World

SHE

holds the infant in her arms
escaping
the heat from
yesterday's struggles
the night's passions
the morrow's fears.

Thank God for this dawn.

"And life pulls so hard,"

says I,
stethoscope around my gleaming neck,
scalpel in hands which
sweat as they
grope for
bits of another's laughter
to
repair my sagging
hopes . . .

Or why need we
wake the muezzin or
sing some matin
for
just another
raggedy day

its foundations eroded

other balms corroded
with
coups or those
election games?

Darling,
open wide your
eye for a stubborn lightness:
the gray fabric rises, and we see
dewy life
under our feet.

Say a word.
Call a name.

Of Gifts and References

The healer knows
his herbs
the farmer
his seedlings
his weeds.

If violet is a color, and
rose a flower:

                              and

violet is a flower, and
rose a color,

then
I'll hang around to

catch
my lessons from
your teacher's lips.

Child,
affection is
cashable
anytime during banking hours,
—when
assets are liquid—

So,
how do I translate
my love,
who has
nothing else to give?

For Kinna II

But
HE said:

Princess,
—and remember royalty
are
made
not
born—

it is not for lack of what
you

could
have
had.

Step up this way and see
these valleys of
green grass that
the winds
the rain and
forever-sun have
rooted so firmly,
fanned up and
leveled down
as though it was a
UN proto-farm.

All that
can,
should,
must be yours,
if I could
drive the malaria from my bones,
accept what I cannot accept,
                                        then
lift
up
my
gun and ...
shoot.

Here on either side of
the great precipice,
time has not begun to get
restless:

the winds are so still
I asked a toucan for a drink, and
he heard me!

Ah,
the land is truly beautiful.

The cattle are healthy,
their udders are full.
And they might even
smile—at milking.

Especially now that their
milk and their
meat go to
                              faraway places to feed
mouths that are less
hungry than our own.

As happens to the potatoes
we till
so slowly
so painfully:
using
ancient implements,
hoeing and
brushing.

Baby,
it couldn't have been
you that I
feared.

The noises

the praises
the blame:
and
affection running as
thin as flax in the hands of a crippled dame,

and
my love,
pawed by
rising expectations and
rocketing inflations,
just
couldn't
fare
better than a fat mouse
before a lean cat.

They say
they mean
us all to

                              walk
                              swim and
                              fly?

What do we do, but
crawl into
corners and die,
who were born without

                              legs
                              fins or
                              wings?

No,
there are choices I

couldn't face
even for
you,

My Little Queen.

Ekunekun

Again she said:

dangerously
I shuttle between two worlds

offering
kolas to his mothers and
spirits to my fathers.

Their reply?

One stared blindly
the other screamed dumbly.

Please,
carry all those tales
of blame to
my doorstep,
who never found the right
corner to stand any pot
yet.

I wish though, that I

could rid me of echoes of a sound
spelling
shame
murder . . .
depths and heights
I would rather not know of.

Like
the day we booed Awisia out of town. We did not
stop at the water's edge. No, not until the
eddies of the river had gleamed over his
footsteps as they slipped off the mushy bed,
did we turn back. And then, only in time to
catch the sheep from the pens hogging on the
week's ration.

They could have organized a nicer way of
crossing
this
junction.

We grieve that in these days of
autobahns
motorways and
complex circles,

it is still the
same
with its
inflexible choices,
on the farm-path or here by
the railings of the
latest
freeway.

Titi,
we have learned the different angles for
raising
waving
dropping the left hand so
the metal,
alloyed and all,
can
catch
the gleam from
less-blessed eyes.

What we need are lessons on
how to stop
laughter from trailing into a
scream.

Shall
my lord
appear

                    in a minute?
                    or two?
                    an hour?
                    ever?

Totems

I
came upon an
owl at the

crossroads blinking with
confusion greater than
mine!

Bird of doom.
Bird of promise.

Fluorescent lighting on a
City cornfield,
Tell the owl of
The changing times.

They-of-the-Crow
cannot
carve out
destinies through
marriage.

Whoever can?

He does
too well by her,

                          and

she always
knows when
starched rags go to swaddle
another's baby.

Dodua of the light palms:
she is hanging out the
last new to dry from its
first washing.

Perch where you can, and

tell your story. They make
us believe that all roofs
cover homes from the rain.

Akua my sister,
No one chooses to stand
under a tree in a storm.

So
you
shall not be the one to remind
me
to keen for the great ancestors and
call to mind the ruined hamlet
that was once
the Home of Kings.

Itu kwan
ma
adze sa wo aa
na
adze asa wo!!!

VI

Kwadwom from a Stillborn Creole Kingdom

Egyeifi's Farewell

Coastal Lady
Coastal Lady,
I could sniff
one hundred miles off, the
one hundred aromas from your
one hundred
soup-pans.

But

don't call my daughter
names.

Watch me
snatching her away
   away
       away.

Coastal Lady
Coastal Lady,
come look for my daughter in the
BUSH.

We may be
feeding on frogs
   frogs
       frogs,

when you come

if you
    ever

come
    ever
        come
            come
                come.

Nourishment

Plentiful supplies of
words that come
pounded
lumpless.
A smooth sauce, strong and sweet.
A well-balanced act.
Talent went into production.

At the prime of its cooking,
such aromas wafted on the
noon air. Ow!

Just grab your
kenkey,
the breezes supplemented
the diet.

There was always something for everybody.
—we could be wrong—

smoked
salted
parboiled. And later,
parfried.

Now
put it before a mongrel and
watch.

Nothing like a dog for a nose.

This type of
mess had a name,
even when it was
only
one night old.

Woaeenn I

The problem therefore,
is
not
aging.

If
graying sets in,
there's always
dy-ing.

Being or not-being is.

Prepare to swallow your pet aversions,

now that
taboos
unmoistened,
chase one another down

                          our willing
                             throats

      with
greasy ease.

VII

Tomorrow's Song

Wanted Urgently For Immediate Employment

Prophets to
update our notions of
doom.

The when of it
the how.

Or perhaps, we need
only ask

any
torturer on a monthly salary?

Scaled to perfection,
               with
spelled-out benefits:
basic vehicle maintenance allowance
chits for fuel
the Sunday waiver
               for all those emergencies,
a faultless pension scheme.

"A necessary part of the state apparatus
you know,"
said the ardent revolutionary-fascist
squashing
regret
               with another swig.

Here
where

nature is so
relentless,
don't look for
footsteps in the undergrowth.

Nothing lasts through
a rainy season—

         and

what the termites
leave
cannot
ever
glue
your good intentions.

She said,

Child,
forgive a mother
who left you adrift "to sink or to swim."

Other mothers have done
the same
      —or worse.

See
how they talk
      and
walk,
sleep   and
weep.

      And
those excel
      who

brew
consoling
infusions
                    which
they serve
in dainty spoonfuls

to cure
                         neither
the fevers from our frustrated desires,
                         nor
the aches of our disappointed hopes:
                         though
potent
enough
                    to
hurt the selves
                    and
the selves' affections.

Then he said:

so child,
you know I meant no harm?

But
quietly through the light evening air
the child replied:

Father,
no one
ever
means
any
harm.

And of course,

neither did you
when you let me
play with the knife around my infant face,

Mother fearing all the while
that

YOU
would have cried,
if

she had said me nay.

Yet
who knows
now,
that

though my sockets
are
empty,
a father's

AND

a mother's
love
illuminate
my way?

In the end
you would only have given the best you had
or

thought
you had:

a few rags from the past,

some solid present pain
political,
persistent,

            with their
attendant
wearisome
economic
woes,

            which
cannot be fully clasped in these
fearfully
shaking
hands.

Too solid to melt under moderate heat,
too firm to even chip
accidentally.

Meanwhile,
take note of
how
the beliefs sit on us
uneasily—
        like all the other ready-made garments:

too small for some
too large for others
too thin for colder bloods,
too thick for warmth.

So
finally,
we
asked:

shall we therefore forget it all,
                    since
no one
has the answer for
the fury of a heatwave in midwinter or
a tropical snowstorm?

No,
we
replied:

we have to
nurse our flickering hopes
through this damp night,

even though
daylight finds us weaker than yesterday.

Who knows,
but in some thicket where time has counted itself out,

some unsane souls are searching for the
roots
which
shall drag
out
the sneeze

that . . .

SOURCE ACKNOWLEDGMENTS

An Angry Letter in January. Coventry, Sydney, Australia, Aarhus: Dangaroo Press, 1992.

Someone Talking to Sometime. Harare, Zimbabwe: The College Press, 1985.

"Me Pilgrim" and "As the Dust Begins to Settle II: An Afterword, Twenty Years On," first appeared in *CLR James Journal* 12, no. 1 (2006).

"An Interrogation of an Academic Kind: An Essay" by Ama Ata Aidoo (pp. 230–33) from *The Legacy of Efua Sutherland.* Edited by Anne V. Adams and Esi Sutherland-Addy. Printed with permission from Ayebia Clarke Publishing Limited, Oxfordshire, UK.

Ghana: Where the Bead Speaks. Edited and designed by Kati Torda Dagadu with an essay by Esi Sutherland-Addy and poetry by Ama Ata Aidoo. Accra: Foundation for Contemporary Art, 2011.

NOTES

THESE DAYS

"Only Flora can attempt to scale Heroes Acre / in a tight skirt and high heels": Credited to Pandi Mutuma in 1985.

someone has plucked / "gracious": The person who used this to describe Mwapa is Yakubu Saaka.

THE NATIONAL CORRUPTION INDEX:
IV. ABOUT SINGLE TREES

Dua kor gye ehum aa; obu: Translation: "A single tree cannot withstand a storm; it breaks."

MOURNING RICCI

Amanfo ei / Hom mbohwe Ricci bi a ose woewu, / ma yereye n'eyi: Translation: "Come, my sister and my kinsman, come, take a glance, and see; someone is claiming to be dead, and he looks like Ricci."

Mo nua Kwabena: Translation: "My brother, Kwabena."

koobi-addict: koobi is salted tilapia, a staple in southern Ghana.

GHANA: WHERE THE BEAD SPEAKS

chevron beads: The Interrogation Beads . . . have been used extensively for trade and barter. Explorers have found them invaluable as gifts for primitive peoples. —*Encyclopedia Britannica*, 2006

IMAGES OF AFRICA AT CENTURY'S END

Whopei! Abae-o-o-o!: Akan exclamations expressing dismay, shock, wonderment, and sometimes, warning. Compare with the following exclamations later on in the poem: "Enfin! Helas!! Mon Dieu!!!" French, translating roughly as "Finally! Alas!! My God!!!"

Ebusuafo: Akan clan hailing normally used during critical times and at other gatherings.

Wekumei: This (Ga, Ghana) and *Ebusuafo* translate directly into one another and are used in more or less the same situations.

THESE DAYS: I
Moboso gya. Mammbohwe wo nkwan m':
Literally, "I only came to borrow a
few live coals from your fire. I never
meant to stare into your soup." In
this case the speaking voice is asking
to be excused. She had meant to
question literally and was not look-
ing for a pretext to get to know other
folks' family business.

THREE POEMS FOR CHINUA ACHEBE:
NEW IN AFRICA: I
Shamwari: Chi-Shona (Zimbabwe)
expression, meaning "friend."

LOVING THE BLACK ANGEL
The Genesis of "Loving the Black
Angel": Although I had known that
I might read at an evening organized
in memory of Alex La Guma and
Ben Moloise by the Zimbabwe Writ-
ers Union, I was not going to try
and write a brand-new poem for the
occasion. How could I? It was only
a week after the hanging of Moloise,
and one had been trained on the
idea that poetry can only issue from
"emotions recollected in tranquility."
Besides, I knew quite well that all we
felt at this murder was RAGE, and
there was no way I, or anyone else
on our side of the battle lines, could
claim then, or ever, that we had
become tranquil enough about it to
"recollect" our emotions and write a
poem. However, that was to change
at dawn on October 25, the day of
the readings. It occurred to me that
if that notion of the genesis of poetry
had never really sounded right to
me before, it definitely sounded
all wrong then. For instance, if we

had organized a wake for our fallen
heroes according to our own customs
and traditions, then those of us who
were recognized by the community
as being poets would definitely be
expected to produce poetry for the
occasion, and our best at that. So in
the morning, I very humbly took
my pen, and the following is what I
was able to do. It should be rough,
this poem, for after all, it did not
emanate from emotions recollected
anywhere near "tranquility."

AN INSIDER'S VIEW
suminado: In Akan, "rubbish dump,"
normally at the outskirts of the
village.

HOMESICKNESS
Fantse: A central coastal dialect of Akan
as identified by the people who speak
it. Non-speakers call it "Fanti." Also
compare *Asante* and "Ashanti."

TWO LETTERS: FAMILY
nuabanyin: "brother"

TWO LETTERS: AFTER AN ARGUMENT
Ndugu: Ki-Swahili meaning "big" or
"respected" brother.

JUST ONE MORE JOB FOR MAMA
Ajumako ampesi wobo kaw dzi: Liter-
ally, "You have to spend money to
eat at Ajumako." Ajumako is a small
rural town in southcentral Ghana
and one of the strategic stops on
the old Accra road, or the old main
east–west artery of coastal Ghana.
It was also one of the points where
the people of that particular region
experienced the trauma of colonial
urbanization with its endemic

meanness of "cash for everything," including meals. In the old days in the villages, a meal was considered "free" because it was prepared from produce that people grew on their farms or from easy gifts from relatives, friends, and neighbors.

Mara mo ndue: Akan. Swearing an oath derived from a personal or collective calamity (as in "my wounded knee") is a way of publicly proclaiming oneself to be speaking an indisputable truth. The accepted convention was that on hearing such an oath spoken, someone present should cry out "due" as an expression of sympathy and understanding. In this poem I am swearing my personal oath and crying out for myself at the same time!

OF LOVE AND COMMITMENT
they say he was a / Kruman you know. / What surprises me / is how they could / have deceived / themselves for so long / trusting a total stranger: An interesting aspect of "the leadership crisis" in post-independence Africa is what one could describe as the "he-is-in-fact-a-foreigner" syndrome. Ghanaians—and other Africans, obviously—are terrific at disowning leaders, popular and otherwise. It was rumored that Nkrumah was from Liberia, Busia from the Ivory Coast, and Acheampong from Nigeria!

NATION BUILDING
Nkondo Kese: In the days when the nations stood on their own feet, every grande dame of the land had several large reed baskets (*nkondo*)

and large brass bowls in which she packed her washed and starched favorite clothes and head ties. According to a woman's whims, these were pulled out and worn on occasions throughout her life. New clothes and other precious possessions were locked away in trunks. However, it was the number of *nkondo* and how full they were which clearly indicated a prosperous life, or not.

A SALUTE TO AFRICAN UNIVERSITIES
Na merepaa wo / Na maye den?: Translation: "What shall I do, if I cursed you? . . . Since my fate is intertwined with yours?"

TWO FOR KOJO: AS THE DUST BEGINS
TO SETTLE—A LONG STORY II
"As for / Him paa diɛ . . .": Ghanaian pidgin expressing bewilderment at a most complicated personality.

GYNAE ONE
"Kwaakwaa" / "Yioo yie" / "Kwaakwaa" / "Yioo yie" / "Alatampuwa" / "Yenyim dzi" / Alatampuwa Yenyim dzi: This is a popular children's play song, usually for hide-and-seek. Much of it happens to be just gibberish. In actual fact, the bit that is clearly meaningful is also heavy with sexual symbolism for little girls, generations of whom sang it blithely enough. They could not possibly have known what it was all about until much later.

REPLY TO FONTAMARA
This poem is a reaction against an earlier personal response to "Love Letter," a poem by Fadrin of Haiti.

HEAVY TRAFFIC

corned beef: Anybody may know what corned beef is, but not everyone would understand what corned beef meant for most Ghanaians, especially those born before March 6, 1957.

FROM THE ONLY SPEECH THAT WAS NOT DELIVERED AT THE RALLY

Amanfuo: This word simply means "citizens," unlike "fellow countryman," a sweetly non-sexist form of public address fairly typical of most African societies. Consider: wananchi, KiSwahili for "children of the soil"; vanavevhu, ChiShona for "children of the soil"; mahlabezulu— Sindebele for "people of this land"; omo-nile— Yoruba for "children of the land"; and so on.

FOR KINNA II

Ah, / the land is truly beautiful. Standing inside parts of the Great Rift Valley, it is very easy to think you are at the beginning of creation. Or at least, in the early days of it. This is especially true of that section that divides the erstwhile White Highlands of Kenya from Lodwar and the semideserts of the north.

EKUNEKUN

Ekunekun: Literally, "husband-husbands," and refers to the notion of playing seriously with the reality of marriage.
Awisia: An Akan word (Twi variant) meaning "orphan." It is a term very much used in early popular Ghanaian music, often pessimistically and dolefully.

TOTEMS

They-of-the-Crow: The Nsona are easily the largest Akan clan. Originally belonging to the Elephant totem, they are now symbolized by the crow and are believed to be witty and generally accomplished in the oral arts. Nsona clanfolk consider themselves to be the greatest people on earth, but since they also tend to be inverterate dreamers, marriage to a Nsona person is often considered by members of other clans to be a most hazardous undertaking.
Itu kwan / ma / adze sa wo aa / na / adze asa wo!!!: Literally, "When darkness overtakes a journey, it does" or "Inescapable reality can only be coped with."

KWADWOM FROM A STILLBORN CREOLE KINGDOM

Kwadwom: A keening, planned, or spontaneous solo, as against a group performed dirge like Ndwonkoro.

EGYEIFI'S FAREWELL

Egyeifi: A praise name for Nkroma (Nkrumah) the ninth-born child, in this case, my aunt who is not herself a ninth-born child but was named after one. Of course, I can't stop folks from associating the poem with Kwame Nkrumah or any other Mkroma/Nkrumah if they want to.

WOAEENN I

Woaeenn: A rather onomatopoeic expression meaning "clear," "crystal clear," or "wide-eyed clarity."

IN THE AFRICAN POETRY BOOK SERIES

After the Ceremonies:
New and Selected Poems
Ama Ata Aidoo
Edited and with a foreword
by Helen Yitah

The Promise of Hope: New and
Selected Poems, 1964–2013
Kofi Awoonor
Edited and with an introduction
by Kofi Anyidoho

The January Children
Safia Elhillo

Madman at Kilifi
Clifton Gachagua

Beating the Graves
Tsitsi Ella Jaji

Gabriel Okara: Collected Poems
Gabriel Okara
Edited and with an introduction
by Brenda Marie Osbey

The Kitchen-Dweller's Testimony
Ladan Osman

Fuchsia
Mahtem Shiferraw

Logotherapy
Mukoma Wa Ngugi

When the Wanderers Come Home
Patricia Jabbeh Wesley

Seven New Generation African
Poets: A Chapbook boxed set
Edited by Kwame Dawes
and Chris Abani
(Slapering Hol)

Eight New-Generation African
Poets: A Chapbook Box Set
Edited by Kwame Dawes
and Chris Abani
(Akashic Books)

New-Generation African Poets:
A Chapbook Box Set (Tatu)
Edited by Kwame Dawes
and Chris Abani
(Akashic Books)

New-Generation African Poets:
A Chapbook Box Set (Nne)
Edited by Kwame Dawes
and Chris Abani
(Akashic Books)

To order or obtain more information on these or other University of
Nebraska Press titles, visit nebraskapress.unl.edu. For more information
about the African Poetry Book Series, visit africanpoetrybf.unl.edu.